NOT HEARERS ONLY

VOLUME II

NOT HEARERS ONLY

VOLUME II

Bible Studies in the Epistle of James

JOHN BLANCHARD

WORD BOOKS
LONDON

Copyright © 1972 by Word (UK) Ltd.

Acknowledgement is made to The Division of
Christian Education of the National Council
of Churches of Christ for quotations from
The Revised Standard Version of the Bible,
Copyright © 1946 and 1952.

Published by Word Books, London, a
Division of Word (UK) Ltd., Park Lane,
Hemel Hempstead, Hertfordshire.

ISBN 0 85009 039 3

Made and printed in Great Britain by
Hunt Barnard Printing Ltd.,
Aylesbury, Bucks.

TO JOYCE

CONTENTS

Foreword

Preface

FOREWORD

by The Rev. Dr. Arthur Skevington Wood, B.A., Ph.D., F.R.Hist.S.

It was the poet and literary critic Matthew Arnold who once declared that 'conduct is three-fourths of our life and its largest concern'. In our permissive society today we need to be reminded that behaviour is not a matter of indifference. Nor must we overlook the derivation of behaviour from belief. It is no coincidence that an age which doubts and even denies the Christian faith is also an age of declining if not disappearing moral standards.

No part of the Bible is more apposite to our contemporary situation than the letter of James, with its constant emphasis on the ethical implications of the gospel. It can be treated as a tract for the times. That is how John Blanchard approaches James, and throughout his exposition we are never allowed to overlook the uncomfortable relevance of these chapters. What comes through forcibly to us is God's word for today.

Like the first volume in the series, this can hardly fail to grip the reader. The style is simple, the analysis lucid, the illustrations fresh, and the insights penetrating. There is nothing academic about the comments. We feel that here is a man who himself has faced life as it is and shares his own experience. Thomas Manton is quoted as saying: 'It is a great fault of some that when they begin to be religious, they leave off to be human.' Mr. Blanchard is in no danger of losing the essential human touch and that is one of the reasons why what he writes is so appealing.

A. SKEVINGTON WOOD
September, 1972.

PREFACE

The Epistle of James has always had a peculiar fascination for me, ever since I first 'discovered' it soon after my conversion. From then on I have been drawn to it again and again. It was one of the first parts of the Bible I went through as a Bible Class leader at Holy Trinity Church, Guernsey in 1958, using, I remember, Canon Guy King's book 'A Belief that Behaves' as a general basis. Later, when I travelled to England as a member of a parish mission team, the Vicar of the Church involved based his daily ministry to the team on the same Epistle, and I began to gain new insights into this great little book.

Some years afterwards, as a staff evangelist with the National Young Life Campaign, I dug a little deeper as I studied it in series with several NYLC branches in the West Country. Then in 1966, on the staff of the Movement for World Evangelization, I led the first of what has since become a large number of delightfully happy houseparties in Europe and elsewhere. Yet again I felt irresistibly drawn to the Epistle of James as a basis for the morning Bible hour, and I found myself returning to the text with a new enthusiasm to discover fresh truths from the familiar words.

In the Autumn of 1968 I accepted an invitation to write a series of Bible Studies for 'Sunday Companion', and found great joy in re-shaping material on the first chapter of James to meet the particular demands of 1,000-word articles for 29 weeks. Those articles, later translated for use in Eastern Europe, greatly added to requests I was already receiving to consider producing a devotional study on the whole Epistle of James in more permanent form. Volume 1 of 'Not Hearers Only' was the beginning of the answer to those requests and I am grateful to the publishers for the opportunity to press on with this further volume.

Anyone even vaguely familiar with the New Testament knows the general line of the Epistle of James, and a glance at some of the titles of books devoted to it confirms the Assessment that is made – 'The Behaviour of Belief' (Spiros Zodhiates), 'A Belief that Behaves' (Guy H. King), 'Make Your Faith Work' (Louis H. Evans), 'Faith that Works' (John L. Bird), 'The Tests of Faith' (J. Alec Motyer). These titles are all trying to crystallise the same truth, that James is a *practical* book, dealing with everyday life for the man in the street. Yet it is not devoid of doctrine, as we shall see when we begin to dig into the text. As Alec Motyer puts it, '. . . the distinctive value of James is his striking grasp of the integration of truth and life'. I agree! – and it is precisely this integration of truth and life that makes James so relevant today. Even as Christians we seem to have an almost incurable tendency to be unbalanced. we either major on accumulating truth, to the neglect of enthusiastic action, or we dash around in a mad whirl of activity, to the neglect of faith and truth. James provides just the balance we need. It is said that when a student was once asked to name his favourite translation of the Bible he replied, 'My mother's'.

'Is it a translation into English?' his friend went on.

'No,' he replied, 'it is a translation into action!'

That, in a nutshell, is James's great concern.

In these studies, I have not sought to deal with critical and technical issues, which are beyond both my aim and my ability. I have therefore assumed, for instance, that the writer of the Epistle was 'James, the Lord's brother' (Galatians 1.19) and that it was written at some time between A.D.45 and A.D.62. I have simply come to the

Word of God with an open heart and sought the Holy Spirit's help in understanding and applying it. In preparing these studies for publication in this form, I have sought, by use of the second person, to retain as much as possible of the personal thrust of the spoken word.

I would like to repeat my thanks to the Council of the Movement for World Evangelization for the privilege of serving the Movement in the ministry of the Word of God, and to Word (UK) Limited for their kind offer to publish these studies. I also deeply appreciate the kindness of my good friend Dr. Arthur Skevington Wood in writing the Foreword to this particular volume. My continued thanks are also due to Miss Sheila Hellberg for her dedication to the task of typing and re-typing the manuscript.

My prayer for this second volume, as for the first, is that the Lord will help writer and reader alike to obey His own clear command, given through James, to be 'doers of the word, and *not hearers only*!'

JOHN BLANCHARD

Croydon,
Surrey,
September, 1972.

Chapter 1

THE DANGERS OF DISCRIMINATION

'*My brethren, have not the faith of our Lord Jesus Christ, the Lord of glory, with respect of persons.*

For if there come unto your assembly a man with a gold ring, in goodly apparel, and there come in also a poor man in vile raiment;

And ye have a respect to him that weareth the gay clothing, and say unto him, Sit thou here in a good place; and say to the poor, Stand thou there, or sit here under my footstool:

Are ye not then partial in yourselves, and are become judges of evil thoughts?' (James 2:1-4)

At first glance this little passage may seem a strange way to begin a book, or even a chapter, yet nothing in the whole of his Epistle is more typical of James's teaching and style. Here are sound doctrine, pastoral warmth, wise counsel and practical commonsense – and all brought to life with the simplest of illustrations. Four things stand out. Let us look at them in turn.

1. *The intimacy that he shared* – 'My brethren' (v.1). James uses this phrase again and again in the course of his letter. In this chapter, for instance, he uses it here in verse 5, and again in verse 14. He seems to use it when he is introducing a new subject, or a new slant on the subject with which he is dealing. Yet there seems to me to be more to it than that. When he calls his readers 'my brethren' he is not just focusing their interest, he is pointing out their intimate relationship as believers.

The Apostle Paul did the same thing as we can see in

that little gem of a book, the Epistle to Philemon. The background would seem to be that Philemon was a wealthy man, living in the city of Colosse. He had in his ownership (and we must use that phrase rather than 'in his employ') a slave whose name was Onesimus. The word 'Onesimus' means something like 'useful', but in fact he was not well named, because it seems fairly clear that he ran away, and if the usual inference drawn from verse 18 is correct, he stole some of Philemon's property at the same time. So at this point in the story Onesimus was a runaway slave, and perhaps a thief into the bargain. If he had been discovered as such he would have been branded in the forehead with a red hot iron as an indication that he was part of the dregs of society. Now where would such a man go? The answer is obvious. He certainly would not go to a small village where every stranger would be recognised. He would go to a big city, where he would be hidden in the crowd. He would want to be anonymous as well as Onesimus! And that is exactly what he did. He went to the great metropolis of Rome, with its teeming masses of people. And then the story takes a dramatic, exhilarating turn, as God stepped into the life of this runaway slave. Just think of it! Here was someone who would be ignored by anyone who knew *anything* about him, yet he was chosen by the Lord, who knew *all* about him! He tried to run away from identification with individual people by going to the city of Rome, and God brought him in touch with the greatest apostle in the Christian church! There, in prison, Paul led Onesimus to Christ. He said of him, 'whose father I have become in my imprisonment' (Philemon 10 RSV), or as we might put it, 'to whom I have given spiritual birth while here in prison'. Then he sent him back to Philemon. That is the human story behind the writing of the epistle. But notice this! In sending Onesimus back to Philemon, Paul says, in verse

16, that the converted slave is returning 'not now as a servant, but above a servant, a brother beloved'. Can you grasp the significance of that? Here was the mighty Paul, an apostle, a Hebrew of the Hebrews, from the tribe of Benjamin, a Pharisee of the Pharisees, a religious blue-blood, a Christian aristocrat. He is speaking of a man who was the scum of the earth, socially speaking. Yet he wraps his arms around him, and calls him 'a brother beloved'. Every barrier, socially and in every other way, had disappeared. We are *one*, he says, in Christ. What is more, remember that he was writing to a wealthy man about a penniless slave, and saying that they, too, are now brothers in Christ! What a lovely, warm grasp Paul had of the same trust that James is underlining here – the intimacy of relationship shared by all born-again believers. Much of what is said in the world today about 'the Fatherhood of God and the Brotherhood of man' is spoken from an empty head and a closed Bible, because the Bible is very particular when it speaks about these concepts. It says that they are only spiritually true within dynamic, personal Christian experience. It is only when we are born again of the Spirit of God that we are made His children and only then do we become true spiritual brothers and sisters. But – and this is the whole point of the illustration from this story of Onesimus – we are brothers and sisters *whoever we are and whatever we have been*. If we are in Christ, then we share this unqualified intimacy of relationship of which James speaks here.

As I travel from country to country I am amazed how often I come to a place I have never been to before only to meet a Christian who comes from my own home town or county, or who knows a friend of mine, or who through some other connection seems immediately to contribute to that great drawing together that there is in being 'in Christ'. I remember saying to one of them, 'It's a small

world isn't it?, to which he replied, 'No, it isn't a small
world, it's just that God has a big family'. What a lovely
touch! – a sense of the intimacy of relationship shared by
all Christians. It is not a small world. It is a vast world,
vast in its size and complexity – but God has a big family
and in it all Christians are intimately bound up the one
with the other. It was precisely this intimacy that James
sensed when he wrote 'My brethren'. Now notice what
follows –

2. *The inconsistency that he saw* – ' . . . have not the faith
of our Lord Jesus Christ, the Lord of glory, with respect
of persons' (v. 1).

We shall see the details of this inconsistency in a
moment, but in its most general terms we could put it like
this: people were saying one thing and doing another.
Now that was something that James could not tolerate.
In fact, the whole thesis of his epistle could be summed
up like this; belief and behaviour must go together. Creed
and conduct should speak with the same voice, in unison –
or perhaps even better, in harmony. However expressed,
they must go together. That is James's concern. He has
noticed a blatant inconsistency among these Christians.
What exactly were its ingredients?

Firstly, *there was a profession of faith* – 'the faith of our
Lord Jesus Christ, the Lord of glory'. We should be better
to translate this phrase 'faith *in* our Lord Jesus Christ'. It
is the same kind of phrase as in Galatians 2:20 where
Paul says, 'I live by the faith of the Son of God'. The
correct translation there (as in the RSV) is, 'I live by faith
in the Son of God'. It was not faith that Jesus had, it was
faith that Paul had in Jesus. James, then, is using the same
formula here. He is speaking to people who made a profession of faith in Christ.

But notice the particular way in which James puts this.
He says that they professed to have put their trust in the

Lord Jesus Christ 'the Lord of glory'. Now it is possible that the words 'the Lord' that appear in that verse were not in the original (you will find them in italics in the Authorised Version), which leaves us with what seems at first look a rather awkward phrase – 'our Lord Jesus Christ of glory'. Rather than join the commentators' carnival over the point, I want us to take the shortened phrase just as it stands, and to see it as a wonderful title – 'our Lord Jesus Christ of glory'. Our blessed Saviour and Redeemer is not just 'our glorious Lord Jesus Christ', – although that is certainly true; not 'the Lord of glory' – though the Bible specifically describes Him in those words in 1 Corinthians 2:8. He is also 'our Lord Jesus Christ of glory'. This is not an adjective to describe Him, but a noun to define Him. Two other New Testament verses with a similar kind of thought will help us to clarify the issue that James is raising here.

The first has to do with His *nature*. It is in John 17:5, and is part of His great high priestly prayer – 'And now, O Father, glorify thou me with thine own self with the glory which I had with thee before the world was'. Now this is a verse about His nature. Humanly speaking, Jesus was born at Bethlehem 2,000 years ago. Yet He existed from all eternity, and He existed from all eternity in the glory of His own divine righteousness. It was not something that He received, nor something that He acquired, nor something that was reflected upon Him. It was not His because of something that He did, or something He became. It was a glory that was His as part of His own divine and eternal nature, a glory before which all heaven and earth is bowed in wonder and worship. The Lord Jesus Christ of Glory!

The second verse has to do with His *nearness*. It has always been a Jewish belief that no man could see God and live. This is exactly what God had said to Moses –

'. . . you cannot see my face; for man shall not see me and live' (Exodus 33:20 RSV). Yet when Jesus was born, when God revealed Himself as Emmanuel ('God with us') notice what John said about Him – 'And the Word was made flesh, and dwelt among us (and we beheld His glory, the glory as of the only begotten of the Father), full of grace and truth' (John 1:14). This is how Charles Wesley put it in his magnificent Christmas hymn:

> *Let earth and heaven combine,*
> *Angels and men agree,*
> *To praise in songs divine*
> *The incarnate Deity,*
> *Our God contracted to a span,*
> *Incomprehensibly made man.*

The Bible says, 'The heavens declare the glory of God' (Psalm 19:1) but man needs something closer than clouds and when the Lord Jesus Christ came to this earth He came as the Lord Jesus Christ of glory, glory that was eternal and divine.

Do you begin to see how precisely all this bears on the point that James is making here? The eternal, glorious Deity of Jesus did not put Him at a distance from men. He was 'separate from sinners' (Hebrews 7:26), but was also very near to them – and He was near to them regardless of their rank, their resources or their reputation. 'Now', James says, in effect, 'your profession is that you are trusting and following the Lord Jesus Christ of glory, the One to whom all honour and glory belong. But He lived among men without fear or favour, and treated all men alike regardless of their rank, their resources, their reputation or their respectability. This is the One in Whom you profess to have faith. But I am afraid that when I look at your lives I see an inconsistency.' That brings us to the next phrase in the verse. Not only was there profession of faith.

Secondly, *there was the practice of flattery* – 'with respect of persons'. Do you see the inconsistency? Faith in our Lord Jesus Christ, the Lord of glory, who lived among men without fear or favour and without any reference to their rank, resources or reputation does not go hand in glove with what James calls 'respect of persons', the practice of flattery.

As everywhere, the meaning and Biblical use of words is vital to our understanding of the Scriptures. Take this word 'respect', for instance. Used in a particular sense, it is something that the Bible both commands and commends. In civil life for instance. Jesus makes it clear that we are to 'render therefore unto Caesar the things that are Caesar's' (Matthew 22:21), while Paul says 'Let every person be subject to the governing authorities' (Romans 13:1 RSV). Titus 3:1 and 1 Peter 2:13 emphasise precisely the same truth. In civil life respect is urged upon us by the Word of God. That, surely, is a word for us today when there is such a spirit of rebellion abroad in the world! – and remember that at least some of these words were written at a time when one of the most godless despots who has ever drawn breath upon the face of the earth was, humanly speaking, in charge of the affairs of men.

Then, too, the Bible urges respect in family life – another area of tragic spiritual and moral breakdown in our world today. Every Christian should give careful consideration to what Paul says in Colossians 3:17–25.

The Bible also urges respect in church life. 'Let the elders who rule well be considered worthy of double honour, especially those who labour in preaching and teaching' (1 Timothy 5:17 RSV). All Christians, and especially all young Christians, should give full weight to those words.

But what about the word James is using here? The phrase 'respect of persons' is in fact one of those enormous compound Greek words that comes from a noun and a verb. The noun is 'face', or 'person', and the verb is 'to lay hold of'. We could literally write it out like this – 'to lay hold of a person's face'. What does that mean? It means to treat a person in a special way, not because they deserve it, but because of something outside of their character, for another, hidden reason – and, by implication, one that is evil. In other words, what James was attacking here was evil discrimination – and 2,000 years later his words have a remarkable relevance! You hardly need me to tell you that. In so many spheres of life today there is a discrimination being practised, often by those inside of the church, which is utterly outside the whole spirit of the Word of God. There is discrimination on the basis of race, a discrimination bitter to the point of blood. There is discrimination on the basis of resources, of money, of material possessions and of religion. There is discrimination on the basis of rank, of office, of position, of influence. I take it to be an indication of our fallenness that in societies where Christ is not honoured, man is invested with the most extravagant titles.

Of course we must get this in balance. I remember on my first visit to Israel going down to the Dead Sea, which is 1,300 feet below sea level. When we reached there the guide turned to us and said 'We are now the lowest people upon the face of the earth'. Perhaps I was over-sensitive that day, but I thought that was going a little too far! Be that as it may, what James is warning us against is the opposite kind of thing – flattery. Someone has said the difference between gossip and flattery is this: gossip is when you say behind a person's back what you would not dare say to their face, while flattery is when you say to their face what you never say behind their back.

With crystal clarity the Bible says, 'To have respect of persons is not good' (Proverbs 28:21), and this is what James is driving home. He is not dealing in this verse with whether the truth is being told. The point here is not dishonesty, but dishonour—dishonour to the Lord. A Christian should never substitute the exercise of flattery for the exercise of faith, nor should he combine them. The Bible says, 'let us give unto the Lord the glory due unto His name' (Psalm 96:8), and when we give to the Lord the glory that is due to Him, then all other deferences should fall into place below that. As Joseph Parker once put it, 'He whose eye is filled with Christ never sees what kind of coat a man has on'.

The intimacy he shared; the inconsistency he saw: now notice

3. *The illustration of this point* – 'For if there come unto your assembly a man with a gold ring, in goodly apparel, and there come in also a poor man in vile raiment; And ye have respect to him that weareth the gay clothing, and say unto him, Sit thou here in a good place; and say to the poor, Stand thou there, or sit here under my footstool': (vv. 2–3).

The Greek word translated 'assembly' is elsewhere translated 'synagogue' in our Authorised Version, although in fact it could be either a Jewish synagogue, a specific Christian gathering or a meeting for church government. Those three interpretations are possible. The principle, however, remains unchanged. The whole point centres on the arrival of two strangers and on their reception. Notice two things about this.

(1) *The appearance*. One of them is described as 'with a gold ring', or as the RSV puts it, 'with gold rings', or as we could even better translate it from the original Greek, 'gold fingered'. He had a gem at every joint, a nugget at every knuckle! He was also clothed 'in goodly apparel',

or, as the RSV puts it, 'in fine clothing'. The point is
obvious. Here was a wealthy man. As for the other visitor,
we are told straight away that he was 'a poor man in vile
raiment'. The word 'vile' means filthy. What a contrast
between these two men as they came into the church. One
in rings and the other in rags! That was the appearance;
now notice

(2) *The approach.* We read this in verse 3. To one of
them there was an invitation – 'sit here'; to the other
there was an instruction – 'stand there'. Notice the difference in the approach! One was offered a seat in 'a good
place'; the other was offered the alternative of either
standing somewhere or of sitting down on the floor, under
somebody's footstool. Here was the discrimination – and
notice carefully on what it was based. We are not told one
of the visitors was a good man, or that the other was a bad
man. What we are told is that one was rich and the other
was in rags. So the basis of the discrimination was finan-
cial. That was the evil of the thing, and from that evil
basis two sins branched out – indulgence of the rich and
indifference to the poor. Not only did they indulge the
rich man regardless of what kind of person he was (pre-
sumably with a view to profiting from him), but they were
utterly indifferent to the poor man *because he was poor*.
That was the only reason for their indifference. It is so
easy to be guilty of that kind of thing. I was at a Christian
holiday centre some years ago, and there was a middle-
aged lady on the staff of the school at which the conference was being held. I forget exactly what her job was,
but it was a very menial task, added to which she was a
very simple person, and, quite frankly not particularly
attractive to look at. During the conference, one of the
speakers asked me whether I had ever spoken to her, and
I had to admit that I had not, although we had been there
perhaps a week already. My colleague than said 'I go out

of my way to speak to her every day. You see, most people pass her by.' I have never forgotten that. I am afraid I have forgotten the lesson sometimes but I have never forgotten the point. 'Most people pass her by.' They ignored her. They were indifferent to her. But not this man. He said, 'I take time to be with her, to talk with her. To make her feel that she is just as important as anyone else here.'

Do you see the point? Is a jewel less precious because it comes in a plain box. Is a soul less precious because it is bound up with what *we* judge to be a limited mind, or an unattractive outward appearance? Carelessness or indifference, especially if they are based on horizontal considerations, are wrong, and could be added to the sins of which the Bible says they should 'not once be named among you' (Ephesians 5:3). Indifference to people is a sin, and indifference to them on the kind of basis we have been examining here is a sin of even greater proportions. Let us beware of it. That is the illustration of his point. Now to the last thing in these opening verses –

4. *The indication of its peril* – 'Are ye not then partial in yourselves, and are become judges of evil thoughts?' (v. 4).

James has illustrated the point, now he indicates the peril. I am sure you have seen those magazine competitions in which children are asked to spot the number of mistakes an artist has made in a picture. Having painted his picture, James now goes on to tell us that there are in fact three things wrong –

(1) There is a *wrong mixture*. 'Are ye not then partial in yourselves.' The RSV puts it like this – 'have you not made distinctions among yourselves'. If that is what James is saying, then it is certainly a very serious fault. It has been said that 'the church must be the one place where all distinctions are wiped out. In the presence of God all

men are one.' That is something we need to remember.
The ground at the foot of the cross is level. There is
seniority in the Christian church but not *superiority*. We
are 'all one in Christ Jesus' (Galatians 3:28) and that is a
oneness not only of integration but of acceptance by the
Lord. In the early days of the Christian church it was
sometimes known for a slave to be served by his master
at the holy communion, as an illustration of the fact that
in Christ they were one. The distinctions had disappeared.
Let us remember that lesson – that the Christian family
is a classless society. Yet the precise truth of James's
point may lie elsewhere, because the word 'partial' is
translated by ten different words in the Authorised
Version. One of them is the word 'wavering' which James
also used in chapter 1:6. If he is using the word in the
same sense here, then his question is – 'are you not wavering?', or 'are you not divided?' They claimed that their
trust was only and utterly in the Lord of glory who Himself treated all men alike regardless of rank, resources,
and reputation. But their behaviour showed that they
were also relying on their ability to gain whatever they
could by discrimination and flattery. They were wavering,
divided.

How we need to examine our hearts here! Are we
living a life of faith? Are we trusting to God to honour
our honesty, or are we resorting to craft and to flattery,
especially with those from whom we hope to gain advantage? Do we trust God for what He is, and men for what
they have? Whenever we do that, then we are using
flattery and not exercising faith. There is a wrong mixture.

(2) There is a *wrong manner* – 'and are become judges'
– or, as J. B. Phillips paraphrases it, 'setting yourselves up
to assess a man's quality'. James accused his hearers of
assuming in a carnal way the right to decide whether a
man was to be received or rejected.

I remember a godly minister who took over a rather dead kind of church. Very soon, he went out doing a lot of personal work, distributing literature and going into public houses to witness for Christ. When the church members got to hear about it they issued him with an ultimatum. Either he stopped this kind of thing or he left the church. Why? 'We cannot have you going into places like that with the gospel; it is like holding revival meetings in Marks & Spencer! If you carry on talking to those people about the gospel and distributing literature to them, do you know what they might do? They might come to church! They might be sitting right alongside us in the pews. I am afraid we cannot have that. Either you stop going, or you leave the church.' Almost unbelievable, isn't it? – and I am glad to say that eventually he did leave that church, and God blessed and honoured his ministry elsewhere.

James hits out against that sort of thing, and returns to the subject later on when he asks – 'who are you that you judge your neighbour?' (4:6 RSV). That is a humbling question. I think I am right in saying that it is impossible for a convicted criminal ever to become a judge in a court of law. Whether that is true or not, it is certainly never right for a forgiven sinner to set himself up as a judge of other men's qualities and characters. To do so is to act in a wrong manner.

(3) There is a *wrong motive* – 'judges of evil thoughts'. The word 'thoughts' is the Greek word 'dialogismos' from which we get our word 'dialogue'. In other words, they tossed the issue to and fro in their minds, they weighed it all up and then they acted in the way likely to do them the most good. The Amplified Bible translates the phrase 'with wrong motives', and Jude's terrible denunciation of false teachers includes their description as 'loudmouthed boasters, flattering people to gain advantage' (Jude 16

RSV). To put money before merit is wrong, and it is born of a wrong motive.

As we close our study of these verses, let us be sure of this. Nothing that James says to you and me is more pungent and penetrating than his insistence that in all of our dealings with our fellow men we should examine our motives, remembering that 'man looks on the outward appearance, but the Lord looks on the heart' (1 Samuel 16:7 RSV).

Chapter 2

THE LORD IS KING!

*'Hearken, my beloved brethren, Hath not God chosen
the poor of this world rich in faith, and heirs of the
kingdom which he hath promised to them that love
him?'*   (James 2:5)

James is now underlining the danger of the sort of thing
described in the previous verses, but before we get to the
heart of what he says here, I wonder if there is a truth
hidden behind those words 'my beloved brethren'. As we
saw earlier, he calls them 'brethren' to emphasise the
intimacy of their oneness in Christ. But now he inserts the
word 'beloved'. Is it because, as his anger rises against
the sin that they were committing, so his love for them
rises in order to meet it, so that his judgement on the
situation is not going to be a judgement against them as
people, it is going to be a judgement against their sin? One
of the most difficult things in the Christian life, is to hold
this balance between hatred of sin and love for the sinner.
It was said of the Lord Jesus that he was 'full of grace and
truth' (John 1:14). Have you ever grasped what a wonderful balance that was? It is so easy to be concerned for the
truth, for dotting every theological 'i' and crossing every
doctrinal 't' and at the same time to fail in the matter of
love. Or we can be so concerned not to hurt anyone, so
concerned to be loving and gentle and full of grace, that
we find ourselves compromising the truth in order to
avoid a disagreement. But Jesus was full of grace *and*
truth, and I believe that James was following His example
here when he called his readers 'my beloved brethren'.

Now what does James have to say in this verse? An

amplified paraphrase would be something like this – 'Listen, by despising the poor out of hand, you are despising some of those whom God has chosen to inherit His kingdom. You have decided to reject some God has decided to enrich.' But beneath the surface of that very simple outline there is a great deal of wonderful truth, as we shall see in a moment.

It has been said time without number that the Epistle of James is a very practical book, and of course that is true. Yet that might lead to a dangerous inference, namely that there are some books in the Bible that are doctrinal, and some that are practical. It is said, for instance, that the two most practical books in the Bible are the book of Proverbs, (which someone has called 'God's transistorised wisdom!') and the Epistle of James. Now that may be true – but what is *not* true is that some books in the Bible are doctrinal and others practical. That is an unscriptural distinction. There are no books in the Bible that are not doctrinal and there are no books in the Bible that are unpractical. As we noted earlier, while there is a great deal in our lives of unbiblical practice, there is nothing in the Bible of unpractical theology. I think we need to recognise that. James is very practical but he is also soundly and thoroughly doctrinal, as we shall see in this very brief verse.

The verse is not a challenge, nor is it a command. It is a statement in the form of a question, and the first part of the statement deals with

1. *The Sovereign's right* – 'Hath not God chosen the poor of this world.'

Bearing in mind what we discovered in verses 1–4, I want you to notice very carefully this one point that will open up your understanding of the whole of the rest of the verse. James argues his case against discrimination, *not* on the grounds that God *doesn't* choose, but on the grounds that He *does*! Remember that James is warning them against the danger of discrimination. He says, 'You are choosing one man, and rejecting another; you are exercising flattery alongside what you claim to be faith'. In this verse, he is going to press home the danger of this discrimination, but he is going to do so not on the grounds that God does not choose but on the grounds that He does. To grasp his argument, we need to realise that he is basing it on a truth which forms part of the bone structure of the whole Bible, and that is God's sovereign right to do precisely as He wills with His own creation. Take that truth out of the Bible and you have a haphazard collection of meaningless words. Let me say three things about this right that God has, the sovereign's right.

(1) *It is incontestable* – 'Hath not God chosen . . .?', James asks. There is no doubt about the answer to that question if you read the scriptures with an open mind. The Bible teems with this truth that so often seems to lie buried under a superficial presentation of the Word of God, even among evangelical people. In the Old Testament, for instance; Moses told the children of Israel 'The Lord your God has chosen you' (Deuteronomy 7:6 RSV); it is said of Levi and of every priest in the Levitical order, 'the Lord your God has chosen him' (Deuteronomy 18:5 RSV); when Saul was announced as king, Samuel said, 'Do you see him whom the Lord has chosen?' (1 Samuel 10:24 RSV); when David was giving testimony before all the people of Israel, he said, 'The Lord God of Israel chose me' (I Chronicles 28:4); at the solemn fast after the rebuilding of the wall of Jerusalem, the people said 'Thou art the Lord the God, who didst choose Abram' (Nehemiah 9:7); later, God told His people 'I have chosen you and not cast you off' (Isaiah 41:9 RSV); God said to Zerubbabel, 'I have chosen you' (Haggai 2:23 RSV).

The same vein of truth runs right the way through the Old Testament from beginning to end and when you come to the New Testament you find precisely the same theme: – Jesus told His disciples 'You did not choose me, but I chose you' (John 15:16 RSV); Paul assured Christians in Greece that 'God chose you from the beginning to be saved' (2 Thessalonians 2:13 RSV); Peter told his readers 'You are a chosen race' (1 Peter 2:9 RSV); and in the last book in the Bible those reigning and rejoicing with Christ are described as 'called and chosen and faithful' (Revelation 17:14). This is the rock on which James builds his case – God has chosen.

A great deal is said in Christian, theological, ecclesiastical circles on the subject of man's free will, but a great deal of it is said without a simple, scriptural understanding that the will is in bondage to the nature, and that the nature of the man outside of Christ is at enmity with God, with the result that will is not in fact free at all, it is held in bondage. It is free, if you like, to operate or to choose within a certain area, but that area is limited by man's sinful nature. That is why when we say that at our conversion we come freely to Christ (and we can legitimately and scripturally say that) we come nevertheless, in the words of the hymnwriter, because

> '*Thou hast made us willing,*
> *Thou hast made us free.*'

When a person comes to Christ they come willingly, they come freely, but they only do so because God in His sovereign grace has overwhelmed their sinful nature at enmity against God and has made them willing and free to come. Until we understand this we have no true understanding of the miracle of a person's salvation at all. Without that truth man always plays a part in his own salvation, by exercising his own free will. But is the truth

THE LORD IS KING!

not this – that the only person in the whole universe with free will is *God*? I put that to you as a very simple statement, but one that is incontestable according to the evidence of scripture. Listen to Nebuchadnezzar, speaking in a Spirit-filled moment of Divine revelation – 'I . . . lifted my eyes to heaven, and my reason returned to me, and I blessed the Most High, and praised and honoured him who lives for ever: for his dominion is an everlasting dominion, and his kingdom endures from generation to generation; all the inhabitants of the earth are counted as nothing; and he does according to his will in the host of heaven and among the inhabitants of the earth; and none can stay his hand, or say to him, "What doest thou?"' (Daniel 4:34 – 35 RSV). There is the sovereign right of God, and it is incontestable.

(2) *It is unconventional* – 'the poor of this world'. What an unconventional choice! You see, human choices are good people, or rich people, or important people, or influential people. That was the whole point of the passage we studied earlier. Two men came into the church. The rich man was received and fawned upon, while the poor man was rejected out of hand. And why was the rich man chosen? Because of his riches, his natural resources. That is the conventional, human, wordly, carnal choice. But God's choice is unconventional. God has chosen the poor of this world. Technically, there are slight variations in the possible meanings of the phrase. It could mean poor in this world's sight – as one translation puts it, 'poor in the eyes of the world'; or it could mean poor by this world's standard – as the Revised Version says, 'poor as to the world'. But those are mere technical details, and they both boil down to the same thing. God has chosen many people that the world would pass by. I used to lead a youth fellowship in Guernsey in the Channel Islands. During the summer

we met every Thursday evening on one of the lovely beaches on the north coast of the island. After a hectic swim, we would pick our teams to play beach cricket. The captains would begin by choosing the fellows, especially those who were good at games. Then they would start choosing the girls. First of all they would choose the girls who were fast runners, then they would reach those who were less athletic. Finally there would be only one person left and she would be told 'you had better go with that lot'. Now I can remember a time when the same person was always left at the end. She was a simple minded girl, and very slow-moving, too, because she was very seriously overweight. She was always the last person to be chosen. In fact, she was not really chosen at all, she was thrown in! Why? Because it was thought that there was nothing whatever that she could contribute to the game of cricket. Yet for all her simplicity, for all her overweight, for all her unattractiveness, *God had chosen her*. She was a Christian. If I can say so reverently and carefully – what an unconventional choice! We never chose her – but God did!

There is a great passage about this in 1 Corinthians 1: 26–29 – 'For ye see your calling, brethren, how that not many wise men after the flesh, not many mighty, not many noble, are called: But God hath chosen the foolish things of the world to confound the wise; and God hath chosen the weak things of the world to confound the things which are mighty; And base things of the world, and things which are despised, hath God chosen, yea, and things which are not, to bring to nought things that are: That no flesh should glory in his presence'.

Notice how that phrase begins. 'Ye see your calling, brethren.' Paul suggests that his readers can see the truth of what he is saying with the naked eye. The Christians only had to look around to see that God had chosen some

notable people, but not many. The people He had chosen
were in the main foolish and weak and base and despised
and 'things which are not'! God's choice is unconventional. God chooses the foolish and they become faithful;
God chooses the weak and they become witnesses; God
chooses the base, and they become believers; God
chooses the despised and they become disciples; God
chooses the world's nobodies and they become the Lord's
nobilities. God's choice is unconventional! As Thomas
Manton put it –

'The first choice that God made in the world was of
poor men, partly that we might not think that wonderful
increase and spreading of the Gospel to come to pass by
the advantage of human power and fleshly aids and
props, but by the virtue of divine grace.'

(3) *It is unconditional*. It is exactly at this point that
James's argument is clinched home. The Bible teaches
at one and the same time that while God *does* choose,
'there is no respect of persons with God' (Romans 2:11).
God chooses without respecting a person's gift, or goodness or anything else. God's choice of people is free and
unconditional. Esphesians 1:4 tells us that His people
were chosen in Christ before the foundation of the world.
Commenting on this truth, C. H. Spurgeon said something like this: 'It is perfectly obvious that in the matter of
my salvation, God chose me, because I would never have
chosen Him. It is also crystal clear to me that he must have
chosen me before I was born, because I am quite certain
he would not have chosen me afterwards!' Let me per-
sonalise the point. If you are a Christian, why has God
chosen you? I have read the Scriptures through from the
first verse in Genesis to the last in Revelation, and I have
not discovered one single reason that the Bible gives us as
to why God should choose us, except for one that leaves
us in adoring wonder at the feet of our Lord Jesus Christ.

There is just one passage that seems to be trying to grapple with the question. Moses is speaking to the people of Israel, and says, 'For you are a people holy to the Lord your God; the Lord your God has chosen you to be a people for His own possession, out of all the peoples that are upon the face of the earth. It was not because you were more in number than any other people that the Lord set his love upon you and chose you, for you were the fewest of all peoples; but it is because the Lord loves you . . .' (Deuteronomy 7:6 – 8 RSV). Even Moses, statesman and spiritual giant that he was, could get no further than that. The Lord set his love upon you because the Lord loved you. Here, in its awesome depths, is 'the love of Christ which surpasses knowledge' (Ephesians 3:19). No man can understand it. To grasp its truth is all we can do, and to do that is to say with the hymn-writer –

> *I stand amazed in the presence*
> *Of Jesus the Nazarene;*
> *And wonder how he could love me*
> *A sinner, condemned, unclean.*

God chooses – uncontestably, unconventionally and unconditionally, and the only hint we have of His reason and motivation is His own great amazing and eternal love. That is something that we will never understand or begin to be able to explain to others. And it is all part of the Sovereign's right.

We now come to the second part of the verse, where James deals with

2. *The saint's riches* – 'rich in faith, and heirs of the kingdom which he hath promised to them that love him'.

It seems to me that James is referring to the Christian's riches in two ways – his riches here, and his riches hereafter. Let us look at them in turn.

(1) *The Saint's riches here.* James says that we are chosen 'rich in faith'. The Amplified Bible renders this 'to be rich in faith', and that puts the point precisely. We are chosen to be rich in (or through) our faith. It is important to notice this. These of whom James is speaking were not chosen *because* they were rich *in* faith; they were chosen to *become* rich *through* faith. Grace is not a reward for faith, but faith is the result of grace. Faith brings the believer's riches into conscious possession. Put another way, faith brings these riches into sight and focus. We can see what our riches are in Christ when we exercise faith.

Just two things about these riches –

(a) *What they cost.* Paul says 'For you know the grace of our Lord Jesus Christ, that though he was rich, yet for your sake he became poor, so that by his poverty you might become rich' (2 Corinthians 8:9 RSV). Grace has been cleverly and helpfully explained as meaning Great Riches At Christ's Expense. Every blessing and benefit possessed by the Christian is one that is given to him at Christ's expense. Our plenty at the cost of His poverty is the teaching of Scripture.

(b) *What they cover* – The Bible says of our benefits as Christians 'In every thing ye are enriched by him' (1 Corinthians 1:5). In every part of life we should look for the enrichment that is ours because we are in Christ. The tragedy is that we fail so often to see this enrichment – and the reason is that we do not put on the spectacles of faith. It is when we put on the spectacles of God-given faith that we are able to see the riches that are ours in Christ in the ordinary moment by moment issues of every-day life. To extend the point, the greater our faith, the more of our riches come into focus. Let me put it this way. Here is someone with just a *grain* of faith, but it is enough to see that Christ died for his sins, in his place. It is enough for him to come to Christ and to trust Him as his Saviour. Now he may go through life with no more faith than that – but he will still get to heaven. It does not take great faith to be a Christian – it takes faith in a great Saviour! A person can be a Christian with no more than a grain of faith, provided it is faith in the Lord Jesus Christ. And of course the poorest in faith, if it is faith in Christ, is more wealthy than the richest person, materially speaking, in the whole world. Do you have that grain of faith in Christ? You may have a great knowledge about Him, some kind of mental understanding of what the Bible is supposed to be saying, but do you have even that grain of faith which has thrown you upon Christ? Have you come to Him and trusted Him and received Him as your Saviour?

Then we can move on from there to *growing* faith; someone who sees a bit more. He sees Christ not only as his Saviour but as his Guide and Helper. He begins to see not only what Christ did for him once for all in His death and resurrection, but what He can do for him now in all of life's difficulties and problems. Someone has said 'an incident is only a problem when I have no resources'; growing faith sees growing resources. A person with growing faith is also growing in grace and knowledge, he is increasingly seeing that Christ not only died for his sins to forgive him but daily and dynamically lives within him, and is therefore able to help him and meet him at the point of his personal need, in all the problems and pressures of life. That is growing faith.

From a grain of faith to growing faith, we come to *great* faith. A person with great faith sees much more. He sees that every circumstance of life is allowed and ordained by God for his own particular benefit and blessing. One only has to read the book of Job to get a fresh grip of this wonderful truth, and there is no incident in our lives that happens outside of the knowledge, ordination, permission and control of the Sovereign God of the universe. But it takes great faith to see that when you have your back to the wall and when your world is crumbling, when you are in the middle of the pain, the pressure, the problems, the difficulties. It is easy enough to speak about it. It falls easy on the ear as sound doctrine – but it is quite another thing to exercise it! Great faith sees riches not only in prosperity but in poverty; not only in health but in sickness; not only in progress but in pressure. This is the faith that sees that God does not allow a single circumstance or event or problem or person or pressure or trial to come into your life without His divine intention that you should be enriched and blessed and strengthened and matured and refined and conformed unto the image of His Son. Spiritual riches are seen through the eye of faith, and it is only great faith that can go through the darkest days with Paul's unshakeable conviction that 'I am persuaded, that neither death, nor life, nor angels, nor principalities, nor powers, nor things present, nor things to come, nor height, nor depth, nor any other creature, shall be able to separate us from the love of God, which is in Christ Jesus our Lord' (Romans 8:38). So much for the saint's riches here. But there are also:

(2) *The Saint's riches hereafter.* James goes on to say that God's chosen people are 'heirs of the kingdom which he hath promised to them that love him'.

In 1952 King George VI died quite suddenly, and I remember vividly our newspaper headline the next day – 'The Queen flies home'. 'But', I thought, 'we don't have a queen. The king just died a few hours ago, and the coronation will probably not be until next year. There is no queen at the moment.' But I was wrong, and the newspaper was right. We *did* have a queen. The King's eldest daughter, Elizabeth was in one of the African countries at the time, and she became our Queen the moment her father died. The coronation had not been held, the official public proclamation had not been made, but she was truly and factually a Queen. And we can reverently say that of those for whom Christ died they are already 'kings and priests unto God' (Revelation 1:6). Their coronation has not yet been held. That will come later. Christians, after all, are 'joint-heirs with Christ' (Romans 8:17) and Jesus said 'My kingdom is not of this world' (John 18:36). Christians may be rejected in this world, but they shall reign in the next. They are kings and priests unto God. Let us note three things about this kingdom.

(a) *It is supreme because of His power.* It is 'the kingdom'. Any reader of history will surely be amazed at the tremendous wealth and power and authority that some men and kingdoms have gathered unto themselves. Individual men have held sway over millions. Yet when you try to hold all of these great political, military, geographical and social conquests in your mind, what do you say when you turn to the Bible, which says of God 'Behold, the nations are like a drop from a bucket, and are accounted as the dust on the scales . . . All the nations are as nothing before Him' (Isaiah 40:15 and 17 RSV). What can we say of the supremacy of the kingdom of heaven? When we are there, we shall be beyond the reach of every trial and difficulty, every temptation and sin, every pain and pressure. All our enemies will have been destroyed, all our fears will have been banished, all our doubts will have been removed, all our hopes will have been realised and all our longings fulfilled. It is supreme because of His power.

(b) *It is sure because of His promise.* It is the kingdom 'which He hath promised'. If there is one thing that is easy to prove today, it is surely the wisdom of Paul's words in 1 Timothy 6:17 that we are not to trust in uncertain riches. Then there is the Old Testament verse that pictures a man seeking to revel in his wealth, and it warns him 'When your eyes light upon it, it is gone; for suddenly it takes to itself wings, flying like an eagle toward heaven' (Proverbs 23:5 RSV). The Bible is so sane in its approach to the subject of materialism. It says that to put trust in 'things' is ridiculous. It makes no kind of sense at all, for riches can disappear as swiftly as an eagle soars into the sky. But the Bible also teaches that the spiritual riches of the Christian are not flying away towards heaven – they are already there! Peter speaks of the Christian as having 'an inheritance which is imperishable, undefiled, and unfading', and he goes onto say that it is 'kept in heaven for you, who by God's power are guarded through faith for a salvation ready to be revealed in the last time' (1 Peter 1:4 – 5 RSV). Not a possibility, not a speculation, but a certainty, spoken by God's word, sealed by God's hand and made sure by His promise.

Soon after Adoniram Judson went out to Burma to give himself to winning the heathen for Christ, he was captured. His enemies strung him up by the thumbs in agonising torture. Then he was cut down and flung into a filthy prison. After a while his tormentors came in to him and said, 'And now what of your plans to win the heathen to Christ?' Judson replied 'My future is as bright as the promises of God'. Every Christian can say the same, because he is the joint-heir of a God-promised kingdom.

(c) *It is sublime because of His presence* 'to them that love him'. The Christian's place in heaven is not a matter of reward, but of relationship. He has promised it to them that love Him. But why do we love Him? John tells us quite plainly – 'We love Him because He first loved us' (1 John 4:19) – and heaven for the Christian is to be for ever with the One he loves most of all, and with the One who loved him before the world was made. Somebody has said that the most satisfying definition of heaven written in the Bible is in John 14:3, where Jesus said 'where I am'. There will be no need for faith in that day, for faith will have been emptied into sight. There will be no need for hope, for hope will have been fulfilled in realisation. But love will be there, and at a depth and a degree never known to us before.

Some time ago I had a letter from a little girl who asked 'Dear Uncle John, I want to ask you a very serious question. When I get to heaven, will I see my white rabbit?' I am not quite sure what I told that little girl, but I am sure I included the line of thought with which we close this study, and that is that when she reached heaven she would be so caught up with an all-consuming view of the Lord Jesus Christ in all of His glory that even the state and location of her white rabbit would assume their correct proportions.

> *The bride eyes not her garment,*
> *But her dear bridegroom's face;*
> *I will not gaze at glory,*
> *But on my King of grace;*
> *Not at the crown He giveth,*
> *But on His pierced hand;*
> *The Lamb is all the glory*
> *In Immanuel's land*

Chapter 3

LESSONS FOR LIFE

'*But ye have despised the poor. Do not rich men oppress you, and draw you before the judgement seats?*

Do not they blaspheme that worthy name by the which ye are called?'   (James 2:6–7)

Taken just as they stand these verses appear very strange indeed, but of course we must take them in context. One of the most helpful things that has ever been said to me concerning the study of the word of God is this; that of every passage of scripture we can ask these three questions – what did it mean at that time? What does it mean for all time? What does it mean to me at this time? You may find that a real help as you read the Word of God.

Let us apply them to these two verses.

Of course they meant something at that particular time. James is making three historical statements. He says in verse 6 'ye have despised the poor'. He then adds – 'rich men oppress you, and draw you before the judgement seats'. He then goes on to say that these same rich men 'blaspheme that worthy name by the which ye are called'. So he makes three historical statements that were obviously true at that time. They are also the outworking of principles that are true for all time. And they certainly embody truth that is relevant for us at this time. In fact it is on this third question that I want to major in this study. What can we learn from these verses? It seems to me that there are three obvious lessons.

1. *There is a peril we must avoid* – 'But ye have despised the poor'.

Notice those first two words—'but ye'. Why are they there? Very simply, James is underlining the fact that his readers' behaviour was in contrast to God's. What has James been saying in verse 5? – God has chosen the poor and He has chosen them to be rich in faith and to be heirs of the kingdom which He has promised to them that love Him. That is what *God* has done – 'But *ye* have despised the poor'. Do you see the point? James was telling them that their actions, their motives, their words, all of these were running contrary to the will and the purpose of God. God did one thing and they did the very opposite. That is the contrast that James is pointing out. Paul supplies the positive teaching on this point when he says 'Let this mind be in you, which was also in Christ Jesus' (Philippians 2:5). That should be the constant concern of the Christian. Our prayer should be in the spirit of A. Cyril Barham-Gould's fine hymn:

> *May the mind of Christ my Saviour*
> *Live in me from day to day;*
> *By his love and power controlling*
> *All I do and say.*

But let us look in more detail at what these Christians had done. They had 'despised the poor'. The Amplified Bible includes the word 'dishonoured' in its elaboration of the word, and this helps to bring out the seriousness of their action. They had dishonoured the poor by rejecting them out of hand, yet they included those upon whom God had placed the highest possible honour – the honour of being 'called the sons of God' (1 John 3:1). In the case that is mentioned particularly, as we saw by way of illustration in verse 3, they decided that the poor man was not worthy to sit with them in church – yet poor men were among those whom God had made 'Sit with Him in the heavenly places in Christ Jesus' (Ephesians 2:6 RSV).

Writing on these verses in his book *A Belief that Behaves* Canon Guy H. King calls his chapter 'The short sighted usher' – and that seems to me to be a very good definition. The usher was short sighted. He saw the two visitors only in their immediate and material context instead of the ultimate and spiritual. He saw them in earthly focus and not in heavenly, and so he was guilty of rejecting someone that God had received. When you take that to its ultimate conclusion there could hardly be a more serious sin. In the parable of the wicked husbandmen, Jesus spoke of His own rejection as a fulfilment of the prophecy in Psalm 118:22 – 'The stone which the builders rejected is become the head of the corner' (Mark 12:10); on the Day of Pentecost Peter told the people that 'God hath made that same Jesus, whom ye have crucified, both Lord and Christ' (Acts 2:36); and later, addressing the counsel when questioned about the healing of the lame man he spoke of 'Jesus Christ of Nazareth, whom ye crucified, whom God raised from the dead'. Here was the same contrast. They acted in one way and it was completely contrary to the way in which God had acted. In rejecting the Lord's messenger they had in this particular case rejected the Lord Himself.

How does all that apply to us? Surely it warns us of a peril that we must avoid, the peril of making judgements purely on superficial, material and worldly levels, and in so doing, of being at cross purposes with the judgements of God. I love the story of the disciples being brought before the counsel because of their enthusiastic evangelism. The wise Gamaliel listened to everything that was said, and, knowing what had been done in the name of Jesus, intervened just as the disciples were about to be condemned. He warned the counsel that they ought to act very cautiously, 'lest you find yourselves fighting even against God' (Acts 5:39 The Living Bible). That principle opens up a huge field of study and possibility. Some of the things I shall mention are not perhaps directly meant by James in context but we can helpfully include them at this point.

In what ways can we 'despise the poor'? One obvious thing we can do is to despise the *poor in number*. Soon after coming into the work of full time evangelism I was asked by one man to conduct an evangelistic campaign in a tiny village in the West Country. With what must have seemed strange enthusiasm I remember taking another evangelist with me, and a soloist too – all for the smallest village I have ever seen in my life! At some of those meetings there were seven people present. One was the preacher, one was the associate evangelist, one was the singer, one was the farmer who had invited us, there were two Christians who had come over from a nearby village, and one other person. So instead of an evangelistic rally we just sat around in a circle, discussed the Word of God together and prayed. A few years later I was at the huge Christian Holiday Crusade at Filey when a strapping soldier came up to me, gripped me by the hand and said 'Do you remember Teign Valley?' With very little sparkle I replied 'Yes, I remember Teign Valley; why do you ask?' 'Because I came to the Lord on the first night of that campaign. You spoke to a little group of young people sitting on bales of straw out in the farmyard. At the close of that meeting I came to Christ. I have been seeking to walk with Him ever since and at the moment I am serving Him in the Armed Forces in Germany. I just wanted you to know that.' Needless to say, I have never forgotten that. To my own shame I have to admit that I despised Teign Valley. I thought it was a waste of two weeks of my time. (Of course we all think our time is very important and so it is.) I despised that little village because it was so poor in number – yet God was at work there in saving power. The Word of God teaches us that we are to be faithful not only in large things, but in little things, too. God sometimes reaps His best and richest harvest in His smallest fields. Never despise the day of small things.

Not only that, but we can despise a person who is *poor in nature*. This takes us a little nearer to the situation James has in mind. Every Christian who knows his Bible must have thrilled to the great teaching of the Lord Jesus in John 4 – words like these – 'whoever drinks of the water that I shall give him will never thirst: the water that I shall give him will become in him a spring of water welling up to eternal life' (John 4:14 RSV); or again – 'God is spirit and those who worship Him must worship in spirit and truth' (John 4:24 RSV), a phrase described as the greatest statement in the Bible concerning the worship of God. Yet this tremendous teaching was first given to a wretched, sin-stained outcast who was fouled with the leprosy of her own lust. Jesus did not despise the poor – He gave His very best to the very worst. The lesson is clear; if we are followers of Christ then we should seek to do the same. Sin is distasteful, sometimes obviously so, but we must never allow the sinfulness of the lost to prevent us reaching them with the Gospel. We must never allow the loathsomeness that sin brings into people's lives to prevent getting alongside them with the saving grace of God.

A friend of mine once belonged to a rather exclusive place of worship. When he suggested to them that they should go on some evangelistic outreach he was told by the elders that they could not do that 'because the Lord hasn't put His name there'. Some time later I was with my friend in a huge secular youth centre. The whole place was in semi-darkness, with language and morals to match. We had gone in to the building to distribute literature and to talk to the young people about the Lord. Remembering his previous experience with the elders he turned to me at one stage and said, 'I don't think the Lord has put His name here!' 'No', I replied, 'but the devil has, and that is why we have come.' There is a great danger in evangelicalism today of becoming middle-class, and of despising everyone we judge to be below our station, below our status, below our quality, below our social level. We despise the poor. There are some people we would be very happy to evangelise, some places in which we would be glad to work for Christ. But are we in danger of despising other people, other places?

Then there are the *poor in need*. There is a danger of being too spiritual in our interpretation of some scriptures. We need to remember that this particular passage is a passage about poverty. It is about the 'have nots' of this world being cold-shouldered by the 'haves'. There is a great danger of thinking that as long as we are preaching the gospel and handing out tracts and evangelising in some way, then we are fulfilling all the Christian service that God demands of us. But that is not true. Of course the gospel is of primary importance, in Christian service, but it is not of solitary importance. The Bible speaks about the cup of compassion, as well as the cup of communion, a cup filled with water as well as one filled with wine. When we despise a situation because of its smallness, when we shrink from getting involved with those whom we feel to be socially outside of our station, when we turn a blind eye to the need of the poor, we are heading straight for a clash with the mind and the will and the judgement of God. That is a peril we must avoid.

2. *There is a pressure we must anticipate* – 'Do not rich men oppress you, and draw you before the judgement seats?'

James now looks at the other side of the coin, and gives a simple reason why these Christians should not toady to the rich. Thomas Manton says, 'James writes these words to show that their practice was not only vain and evil, but mad and senseless!' These rich men were the very ones who hauled the Christians in to court. They 'oppress you', James said. Literally, we could translate this 'they abuse their power against you', and it is significant that the only other use of that particular word in the Bible is in Acts 10:38 where we read that Jesus 'went about doing good, and healing all that were oppressed of the devil'. We are not told of any precise cases that James had in mind here, but it is not difficult to find evidence to prove his claim. I once went through the Acts of the Apostles marking out the subject of the persecution of Christians, and linking the references together. I began in chapter 2, verse 13 with the word 'mocking' and I went right on to chapter 26, verse 24 where Festus said to Paul, 'you are mad; your great learning is turning you mad' (RSV). Altogether I discovered about 50 instances of Christians being persecuted for their faith, by beatings and stoning, by scourging and imprisonment, by slander and evil speaking of every kind. And often this was done by rich men or by leading people. Why? Why were Christians oppressed by the rich men of their day? We can list three obvious reasons.

(1) *The gospel hit at their positions.* Again and again we read that the Jews stirred up trouble against the disciples because their positions were in danger, because this wonderful good news of salvation through faith, and through faith in Christ alone, hit at the positions held by the priests and others. All the rituals and ceremonies and sacrifices were swept away by the glorious gospel of the Lord Jesus, and when the gospel hit at their position, then they hit at those who were preaching it.

(2) *The gospel hit at their pocket.* There are some obvious examples of that. At Philippi, for instance, when Paul exorcised an evil spirit from a girl with a spirit of divination, we read that 'when her owners saw that their hope of

gain was gone, they seized Paul and Silas and dragged them into the market place before the rulers' (Acts 16:79 RSV). Then there was the occasion at Ephesus, that great centre for the worship of the goddess Diana. The Bible tells the story of the silversmith Demetrius, a maker of silver images who 'brought no little business to the craftsmen' (Acts 19:24 RSV). Notice that! They made money out of a false religion, and when the gospel was preached Demetrius realised that this was going to eat into their profits. He got the craftsmen together and warned them that because of Paul's preaching 'this our craft is in danger to be set at nought; and the temple of the great goddess Diana should be despised, and her magnificence should be destroyed' (Acts 19:27). I think that is a most illuminating phrase. Demetrius saw two tremendous dangers – the first was that they would lose money and the second was that the great goddess Diana would be despised. Notice the order! The result, we read, is that 'full of wrath' they dragged two of Paul's companions, Gaius and Aristarchus, into the amphitheatre to face a public trial. Why? Because the gospel hit at their pockets, and because of that the gospel and those who preached it must go.

(3) *The gospel hit at their pride.* Many of the early Christians were poor people, and it has been said that many of them, before their conversion, contracted debts with rich money lenders. Now their new profession of liberty would anger the lenders, who saw things only in terms of materialism. As a result the screw would be turned and the oppression of the poor by the rich was common and callous. Corrupt judges in those days were very often 'in rich men's pockets', and the result was often terrible pressure brought to bear on the poor Christians. They were despised and oppressed not only because the gospel hit at men's position and hit at their pocket but because it hit at their pride.

Surely the application of the latter to us is clear. In Galatians 5:11 Paul speaks of the 'offence of the cross'. He says that his unwillingness to compromise the cross is the reason that he is being persecuted, and that points out a most vital truth for us. It is a principle we must recognise because it points to a pressure we must anticipate. The preaching of the cross on our lips, or the principle of the cross in our lives, will always be an offence to the natural man. Man wants the results of the cross but never its requirements. He wants the happiness that it brings, but not the holiness that it demands; the comforts that it offers, but not the cost that it involves. Any preaching and way of life that takes all of the pride, arrogance, wealth and authority of man and lays it in the dust is never likely to be universally popular. There is a pressure we must anticipate. If we preach the kind of message and live the kind of life that takes man down off his self-made pedestal and lays him in the dust before an Omnipotent and Sovereign God, then it is not going to be popular, and we are going to be pressurised. The Lord Jesus made that so clear – 'If you were of the world, the world would love its own; but because you are not of the world, but I chose you out of the world, therefore the world hates you. Remember the word that I said to you. "A servant is not greater than his master". If they persecuted me, they will persecute you; if they kept my word, they will keep yours also' (John 15:19–20 RSV). There is the pressure that we must anticipate. It is impossible at one and the same time to walk closely with the Lord and to be comfortable in the world in which we live today. John Newton, the converted slave trader, once said this – 'Can the servant expect or desire peace from the avowed enemies of his master? We are to follow his steps; and can we wish, if it were possible, to walk in a path strewed with flowers when His was strewed with thorns?'

There is a pressure we must anticipate. Of course we are not to excite this, but we are to expect it.

3. *There is a profanity we must abhor* – 'Do not they blaspheme that worthy name by the which ye are called?'

This was the climax of their crime. They not only dragged the Lord's people into court, but they dragged the Lord's name into contempt. There are specific incidences of this mentioned in Acts and it is not difficult to imagine many more cases where the hatred of Christians led men to blaspheme that worthy name that the Christians bore. No wonder James infers that it was the height of folly for Christians to toady to these men to whom Christ was just a swear word! Now what are the specific things we can gain from this final phrase? Two things stand out –

(1) *A great dignity* – 'that worthy name by the which ye are called'. The word 'worthy' (obviously of the Lord Jesus) is the Greek word 'kalos', which is often translated 'good'. It means exalted, or better than others, and James's use of it here reminds us that the Lord Jesus has 'a name which is above every name' (Philippians 2:9). But what of this other little phrase – 'by the which ye are called'? The Amplified Bible says, 'by which you are distinguished and called', while another translation renders it, 'the name which was called upon you'. It might help us to go back to Genesis 48:16 where Jacob, the dying old man calls his sons together, lays his hands upon the heads of Ephraim and Manasseh and says, 'let my name be named on them'. Now the phrase we have here in James might be translated in rather the same way as 'the worthy name which was called upon you'. Perhaps the reference is to their baptism; certainly Christians were children of God, and certainly the command was to baptise them 'in the name of the Father, and of the Son, and of the Holy Ghost' (Matthew 28:19); so perhaps we are exactly at the point that James is making here. If so, what he is saying is that the rich and

ruthless men who were despising the early Christians and dragging them into the law courts, were also blaspheming that worthy, triune name of the living God, the name which was called upon the Christians when they made their open profession of faith.

The other use of this kind of phrase is in marriage, where the wife takes the name of the bridegroom, and perhaps there is a vein of truth here, for after all the church is the bride of Christ. But whatever the picture, the principle is absolutely clear. Christians bear the name of Christ and they ought to reveal His nature in their daily lives. We should live and speak and act in such a way that we reflect something of the wonder of 'that worthy Name'. Our witness should be so clear and definite that it ought to be perfectly obvious whether or not we belong to Christ. If there are people who walk with us, work with us, live and play with us day by day, and they have no knowledge of the fact that we belong to Christ, then there is something deficient in our discipleship. We ought not to have to walk around with enormous Bibles in order for people to know that we are Christians. People ought to know it. They ought to sense it. They ought to feel it. There ought to be something about the very presence of God in the place when we are there. There is a great dignity here – that worthy Name which was called upon you. In the words of that magnificent chorus –

> *His name is wonderful*
> *His name is wonderful*
> *His name is wonderful, Jesus my Lord.*
> *He is the Mighty King,*
> *Master of everything,*
> *His name is wonderful, Jesus my Lord.*
> *He's the great Shepherd,*
> *The Rock of all ages,*

Almighty God is He;
Bow down before Him,
Love and adore Him;
His name is wonderful,
Jesus my Lord.

(2) *A great danger.* 'Do not they blaspheme . . . ?' James asks. Incidentally, that surely settles the question as to whether these people were Christians or not, because no Christian would openly blaspheme the name of Christ. It may therefore seem that of all the sins mentioned in the Bible this is the one that it might be thought totally unnecessary to warn Christians against. Yet, I believe that there is a double danger that even as Christians we might be guilty of blasphemy – the first is by unguarded lips and the second is by ungodly lives.

(a) *Unguarded lips.* The New Bible Dictionary defines blasphemy as 'an act of effrontery in which the honour of God is insulted by man' and what we must realise as Christians is that God is insulted not only by cursing, but by being casual in holy things. It grieves the Holy Spirit when Christians slip so easily into light-weight conversation about God, when they give the impression that they are pally with the Deity, when they can crack jokes about God and make flippant remarks about the Lord we adore, and casual claims about what God has said and done. That is blasphemy. There is a verse in Jeremiah 23:32 which accuses false prophets of causing God's people to sin 'by their lies *and by their lightness*'. Do we cause people to stumble because of our lightness? We live in an age of informality. The cult of the casual is one of the most widespread phenomena in the world today. Today's world is casual in its dress, in its habits, in its language, and in its morality. We are casual in our inter-personal relationships and we are in danger of being casual about God. And let it be said very carefully that no section of the Christian church is in a greater danger in this regard than those who are proud to call themselves evangelicals. The High Churchman, the ritualist, the sacramentalist is not in nearly the same danger. He has a great sense of awe and mystery and seriousness and soberness when he comes to think and speak about God. But we evangelicals have got rid of the ritual, we have got rid of the ceremony; and at the same time we have got rid of the mystery, we have got rid of the awe, and we talk about God casually. Is there not a great danger here? The Bible teaches us that we can come freely into the presence of God but not flippantly. 'Oh magnify the Lord with me' the Psalmist says, 'and let us exalt His Name together' (Psalm 34:3).

(b) *Ungodly lives.* Many years ago a German philosopher called Friedrich Nietzsche became interested in Christianity. He began to move among Christian people, to listen to what they were saying, to watch what they were doing. After a long while he came to this conclusion – 'These Christians will have to look a lot more redeemed before I can believe in it'. So Nietzsche went back to his philosophy and his searching – and eventually became the spiritual father of Nazism and the forerunner of the God-is-dead theology. Now that is admittedly an unusual case, but it is not a unique one. As far back as Romans 2:24 Paul was able to say of some Christians that 'the name of God is blasphemed among the Gentiles through you', while in writing to Timothy he told Christian servants to behave in such a way 'that the name of God and His doctrine be not blasphemed' (1 Timothy 6:1).

We should never under-estimate the power of our personal influence, and especially of its effect in spiritual terms. We need to guard against that inconsistency of life that turns people away from Christ, or that becomes a factor in bringing them to a position where they blaspheme the Name we bless. No verse in the whole Bible is more challenging than these words of Jesus 'He who is not with me is against me, and he who does not gather with me scatters' (Matthew 12:30 RSV).

To be an accessory before the crime is a serious offence in law – and it is even more serious in the realm of grace! The Rev. H. R. L. 'Dick' Sheppard, of St. Martin-in-the-Fields, London, that renowned 'soap-box' orator at Hyde Park Corner, once said 'If anything emerged from that ancient war of words it was this, that the greatest hindrances to the spread of Christianity are the unsatisfactory lives of professing Christians'. In the matchless Sermon on the Mount, Jesus made our responsibility clear – 'Let your light so shine before men, that they may see your good works and give glory to your Father who is in heaven' (Matthew 5:16 RSV). Here is the life at which we should aim; one that does not drive men from the Bible, the church, Bible, prayer, Christ – but one that draws them to them – a life in which we 'adorn the doctrine of God our Saviour in all things' (Titus 2:10). It was exactly this longing that was expressed by Joachim Lange in these words, translated by John Wesley:

> *Lord, arm me with Thy Spirit's might,*
> *Since I am called by Thy great name;*
> *In Thee let all my thoughts unite,*
> *Of all my works be Thou the aim:*
> *Thy love attend me all my days,*
> *And my sole business be Thy praise.*

Chapter 4

THE CHRISTIAN AND GOD'S LAW – I

'If ye fulfil the royal law according to the scripture,
Thou shalt love thy neighbour as thyself, ye do well:
  But if ye have respect to persons, ye commit sin, and
are convinced of the law as transgressors.
  For whosoever shall keep the whole law, and yet
offend in one point, he is guilty of all.
  For he that said. Do not commit adultery, said also,
Do not kill. Now if thou commit no adultery, yet if thou
kill, thou art become a transgressor of the law'.

(James 2:8–11)

In these verses James develops his theme of condemning
unworthy, unbiblical, ungodly discrimination against men
on purely horizontal considerations. The gist of verses 8–11
could be paraphrased like this: If you carry out in your
daily lives all the commandments that the scripture lays
upon you in terms of your relationships with your fellow
men; in other words, if you love your fellow men in the
same way as you love yourself, you are certainly doing a
very fine thing. But if you discriminate against some men,
then the law convicts you quite clearly as being sinners.
Indeed, if a man is perfect in his life except for one point
then that man is guilty of breaking the law of God, which
stands as an entirety, not as a collection of bits and pieces.
The God who said, 'Do not commit adultery' in the same
breath said, 'Do not kill'. So if a man does not commit
adultery but kills, or vice versa, then he is still guilty of sin
and is a transgressor of the law.

Although we shall separate them for the purpose of

these studies, the next two verses in the Epistle (verses 12 and 13) form part of the same passage, and the whole section (verses 8–13) could be called 'The Christian and God's law'. This first group of verses (8–11) tell us how the law is described, and then shows us what the law discloses.

1. *How the law is described* – 'If ye fulfil the royal law according to the scripture, Thou shalt love thy neighbour as thyself, ye do well' (v. 8).

All the truth in this section stems from the way in which this law is described – and it is described as 'the royal law'. In what ways can that be said to be a valid description of God's Word? Let us notice just three –

(1) *Its source is royal.* At one point during our Coronation Service a Bible is handed to the incoming monarch with these words – 'We present you with this Book, the most valuable thing this world affords. Here is wisdom, this is the Royal Law. These are the lively oracles of God.' Notice that! – 'the Royal Law'. When we hold the scriptures in our hands we are holding a Book whose source is royal. It has God as its Author. Nearly 4,000 times in the Old Testament alone; 700 times in the Pentateuch, the most disputed part of the scriptures; 40 times in one chapter the writers claim to be speaking God's word. 'God spoke', 'the word of God came', 'God commanded', 'thus saith the Lord', 'the Lord spoke these words' – this is the language of the Old Testament from beginning to end. Now either that is true or the Bible is not only a good book, but is certainly the worst book, in moral terms, that has ever been written. If a book tells us 4,000 lies, and, moreover, 4,000 blasphemous lies, about its origin, then it is thoroughly evil and downright blasphemous. When we come to the New Testament, we discover that it contains approximately 600 quotations from the Old Testament, all of them taken as authoritative. Not one of them is questioned. And when the New Testa-

ment comes to speak about itself, listen to the terms it uses. Paul says, '. . . the things that I write unto you are the commandments of the Lord' (1 Corinthians 14:37). John says, 'This then is the message which we have heard of Him' (1 John 1:5). In the plainest possible way the Bible claims to have God as its Author and Source – it claims to be a Royal Law.

In the People's Bible, published in 1895, Joseph Parker said this – 'The Bible stands alone. Other books are as trees which men have planted, and trimmed, and pruned with periodic care; but the Bible belongs to that forestry of thought, event, direction and sovereignty which human hands never planted – a church built and aisled and lighted in a way beyond the ways of man.' That is wonderful oratory, and glorious truth! The Bible stands alone. Its source is royal.

(2) *Its subjects are royal* – 'If ye fulfil the royal law . . . ye do well' (v. 8). Of course God's spiritual law is for every man, and we need to recognise this very clearly. God's law is meant to be relevant to every single person who draws breath on the face of the earth, regardless of their knowledge or experience of God. Every individual on the globe must reckon with the spiritual law of God as contained in the Holy Scriptures, just as every man in the world must reckon with the law of gravity. *Every man*, whether he is a believer or an unbeliever, a religious man or an infidel. God has material and scientific laws for the government of this universe and every man must reckon with them. No man can say, 'I do not believe in God and therefore I will have nothing to do with the law of gravity'. In the same way, every man must reckon with God's spiritual law. The man who defies this Book, the man who ignores it, the man who lives his life contrary to its teachings, is heading for certain spiritual disaster – because this is the Law of God. It cannot be ignored. No man can

set it aside. Yet the Bible has a different purpose for
different people. For unbelievers, it is to help them to find
Christ; for believers it is to help them to follow Christ.
Let us just notice these two points in passing.

(a) *For unbelievers the Bible helps them to find Christ.*
Listen to Paul in Galatians 3:24 – 'Wherefore the law was
our schoolmaster to bring us to Christ, that we might be
justified by faith'. Notice the past tense – 'the law *was* our
schoolmaster . . .', in other words before we were converted. And then what a wonderful statement of the purpose
of scripture for the unbeliever – 'to bring us to Christ'.
The scriptures' task was to reveal sin, to show us our
awayness from God, to show us the hopelessness of our
case, to show us that we could never behave or think our
way to God – and then to show us that only in Christ could
we be justified freely by His grace. The Bible is for unbelievers to find Christ, and to become children of the King.

(b) *For believers the Bible helps them to follow Christ.*
Notice the very next verses in Galatians. 'But after that
faith is come, we are no longer under a schoolmaster. For
ye are all the children of God by faith in Christ Jesus'
(Galatians 3:25–26). Paul does not say that having become
Christians we can throw the Bible overboard as of being
no value whatever. It was the Old Testament that Paul
described as 'our schoolmaster to bring us to Christ' – but
it was also of the Old Testament that Jesus said '. . . it is
they that bear witness to me' (John 5:39 RSV). Even in
the reading of the Old Testament the Christian is taught to
follow Christ. If there is anything that should convince
us that the Bible is a unity, that it is one Book from beginning to end, it is that the Old Testament scriptures are used
by the Spirit of God to help the Christian to follow Christ
day by day. Of course when we come to the New Testament the picture is even clearer, because we have the
straight-forward life and teaching of Christ and His

apostles. Peter says – 'Christ also suffered for you, leaving you an example, that you should follow in His steps' (1 Peter 3:21 RSV). Every part of the Bible from Genesis to Revelation, the law and the gospels, Psalm and prophesy, narrative and epistles, are written for the blessing and benefit and guidance and comfort and encouragement and enabling of God's people, that they might be 'conformed to the image of His Son' (Romans 8:29 RSV). Paul says plainly that 'All scripture is given by inspiration of God, and is profitable for doctrine, for reproof, for correction, for instruction in righteousness' (2 Timothy 3:16). And for what purpose? – 'That the man of God might be perfect, throughly furnished unto all good works (2 Timothy 3:17). Its subjects are royal!

(3) *Its standards are royal* – 'If ye fulfil the royal law according to the scripture, Thou shalt love thy neighbour as thyself . . .' (v.8).

When Jesus was asked which was the first commandment of all He linked two scriptures together in His reply – 'Hear, O Israel: The Lord our God, the Lord is one; and you shall love the Lord your God with all your heart, and with all your soul, and with all your mind, and with all your strength . . . You shall love your neighbour as yourself', adding 'There is no other commandment greater than these' (Mark 12:29–31 RSV). Of course Jesus did not mean that there were other commandments *less* important than these. The explanation is in Matthew's version which adds – 'On these two commandments depend all the law and the prophets' (Matthew 22:40 RSV). In the first part of His reply, Jesus was summarising the first four of the Ten Commandments. These have to do with our dealings with God. The second part of His reply was a summary of the last six commandments, which have to do with our dealings and relationships with one another. Now do you see what James is doing in the verse we are studying? He is taking Jesus's summary of the last six commandments – 'You shall love your neighbour as yourself' – and calling it 'the royal law' concerning our relationship one with another. 'You shall love your neighbour as yourself' is a summary of every demand the Bible makes upon us concerning our relationships with one another – and what a royal standard that is!

Remember that when the commandments were given men did not live in rows of semi-detached or terraced houses. It was not just a case of loving the person next door. When Jesus told the story of the Good Samaritan, he made it crystal clear that our neighbour might well be our sworn enemy. The standard that Jesus sets for us is 'that you love one another as I have loved you' (John 15:12 RSV).

But what does the Bible mean when it says that we are to love one another? 'Love' is a word that is grossly misused and misunderstood today, and our only dependable source of explanation must come from the Bible. I have studied this word very carefully in the scriptures and I have come to the conviction that what love means in terms of our relationships one with another is this: whatever a person does, whatever a person thinks, whatever a person says, whatever a person believes, however much they might despise you, and abuse you and criticise you, to love them is to act towards that person in a way that is deliberately calculated to bring about their highest good and their greatest blessing. That is the biblical meaning of love. No greater demand is laid upon us in terms of personal relationships than that we should love one another and nothing more clearly reflects the mind of Christ. When we do that, the standard of our living begins to rise.

In Ernest Gordon's book *Through the Valley of the Kwai* he describes a Japanese prisoner of war camp in Burma, and in one part of the book he tells the difference between conditions there at Christmas 1942 and Christmas 1943. In 1942 the camp was a sea of mud and filth. It was a scene of gruelling, sweated labour and brutal treatment by the Japanese guards. There was hardly any food, and the law that pervaded the whole camp was the law of the jungle, every man for himself. Twelve months later, the ground of the camp was cleared and clean. The bamboo bed slats had been de-bugged. Green boughs had been used to rebuild the huts and on Christmas morning 2,000 men were at worship. Why the difference? Why the jungle one year and Jesus the next? In between the two Christmas days, one man had shared his last crumb of food with another man who was also in desperate need. Then he had died. Amongst his belongings they found a Bible. Could this be the secret of his life, of his willingness to give to others and not to grasp for himself? One by one the prisoners began to read it. Soon the Spirit of God began to grip their hearts and change their lives and in a period of less than twelve months there was a spiritual, moral and practical revolution within that camp. It was lifted from disgrace to dignity by the Word of God whose standards are royal. When the Bible begins to be lived, men begin to be lifted.

Here, then, is a Book whose source is royal, whose subjects are royal and whose standards are royal. That is how the law is described.

2. *What the law discloses* – 'But if ye have respect to persons, ye commit sin, and are convinced of the law as transgressors.

For whosoever shall keep the whole law, and yet offend in one point, he is guilty of all.

For he that said, Do not commit adultery, said also, Do not kill. Now if thou kill, thou art become a transgressor of the law' (vv. 9–11).

In these verses, the law of God discloses two things –

Firstly, the record of our guilt. These verses are a Charge Sheet, and all of our names appear on it. It is a catalogue of crime, in which we are all involved. We will see our involvement if we separate James's teaching here into four headings –

(1) '*Do not commit adultery*' (v. 11). This, of course, is the seventh of the Ten Commandments, quoted by James from Exodus 20:14. Jesus called His age 'an evil and adulterous generation' (Matthew 12:39), and 2,000 years later His words are a precise description of our 20th Century world. If we were to gather from all available sources the statistics made available concerning the moral decline of the world in which we live then I believe we would bow our heads in shame as being part of a generation wallowing in an immorality perhaps never equalled in the history of the world. Let me give you just one example of the kind of thing I mean. When I was originally preparing this particular study there was an article in the Reader's Digest on the subject of venereal disease in Britain. It disclosed that every day in Britain nearly 50 teenagers were contracting syphilis or gonorrhoea; that the yearly total of these diseases had trebled in the previous decade; that in 1966 there were 37,000 new cases of gonorrhoea in Great Britain; that the country's second commonest infectious disease next to measles was venereal disease; that in 1968 200,000 new patients were attending venereal disease clinics; and that 200 of those clinics could not cope with the numbers who were coming to them. And this is only one small part of the moral cancer that is eating away at our country. Yet before we catch up our righteous robes and say that at least we are free from that sort of thing, that at least we have never committed the act of physical adultery, let us remember that Jesus made it crystal clear that if a man looked on a woman with lust he was guilty of adultery in his own heart. Now we are so

constituted that the sin of lusting by looking is one that by and large lies at the door of men and not women. But make no mistake about it, the woman's contribution to that situation is by no means a small one. No Christian woman or girl should ever act or speak or dress or behave in the kind of way that is calculated or likely to contribute to the sin of adultery in the eye and in the heart of the man.

(2) '*Do not kill*' (v. 11). This is the sixth of the Ten Commandments, and is quoted from Exodus 20:13. In the eyes of some, this is the worst crime of all, and so it is one from which most men would claim innocence. But again we remember the interpretation that Jesus put upon it, when He said that a man who was angry with his brother without a cause was likewise guilty of murder. Are we innocent now? Dr. Ligon, in his book *Psychology of the Christian Personality* said, 'If the psychologist were asked to name the two major sins from his point of view, he would probably name fear and anger. They form the basis of most of our unhappiness. They are impossible to integrate into a healthy personality.' Fear and *anger*. There is perhaps not one of us who can claim to be free from that charge.

(3) '*but if ye have respect to persons, ye commit sin, and are convinced of the law as transgressors*' (v.9). Adultery, murder and now 'respect of persons' or, as the RSV puts it, 'partiality', and all named together in the same passage. James has said many things about partiality, or respect to persons so far. Now he bluntly calls it sin. You are 'convinced of the law' ('convicted by the law' RSV) he says, if you show partiality. You may not commit adultery, you may not commit murder, but if you show partiality towards people, if you discriminate on horizontal grounds, then you are guilty of sin. You are convicted by the law. And so are we, both *specifically* and *generally*. Specifically, of course, in the plain words of the Old Testament

law – 'You shall do no injustice in judgement; you shall
not be partial to the poor or defer to the great, but in
righteousness shall you judge your neighbour' (Leviticus
19:15 RSV). The law specifically convicts us. But the law
also convicts us generally. What *was* the law, the royal
law, concerning relationships with one another? 'You
shall love your neighbour.' And what is love? It is not to
fawn upon the rich man for unworthy motives. That is
dishonesty. And it is not to be indifferent to the poor man.
That is unkindness. The whole teaching of the law is that
we love our neighbour regardless of rank and reputation.
If we do either of these things, we are convicted by the
law as transgressors.

(4) '*For whosoever shall keep the whole law and yet offend
in one point, he is guilty of all*' (v. 10). The word 'offend' is
the word used in the AV of Jude 24 where we read that the
Lord is able 'to keep you from *falling*', or literally 'even
from stumbling'. The word means a very small slip-up,
and James says that to commit even one 'little' sin is to be
'guilty of all'. Obviously such a man is not guilty of
breaking every part of the law. What James is saying is
that he is guilty of not keeping every part. If you are
guilty of one little sin, then the whole law lies broken,
because the law of God is an entity. A man cannot pick
and choose his virtues. The question of whether we can
stand on our own two feet before God without the cross
and without Christ and without His forgiveness is not
whether there are many laws we have kept, but whether
there are any laws we have broken. There is a word here
for those outside of Christ, the unconverted, the unsaved.
The question of whether you will be able to face God on
the basis of the kind of person you have been, does not
rest on whether there are many laws you have kept, but on
the matter of whether there are any you have broken. If
there is one, then you are guilty of all. 'For whosoever

shall keep the whole law and offend *in one point* he is guilty of all.' The law of God is not like a pile of stones, from which you can take one away and not notice the difference. It is like a pane of glass; one scratch and the whole thing is ruined. One broken link and the whole chain is broken; one puncture and the tyre is flat; one rip and the suit is ruined; one leak and the vessel is sunk. One sin and a man is in hell. That is what the scripture teaches, in the clearest possible way – 'For all who rely on the works of the law are under a curse; for it is written, "Cursed be every one who does not abide by *all things* written in the book of the law, and do them"' (Galatians 3:10 RSV). Notice those words 'all things'! If a man is relying on his good works to please God and to be saved, then he is under a curse, because the only way in which he could conceivably please God is by keeping *all things* in the book of the law. This is what a man is up against when he tries to justify himself in God's sight.

These verses, then, are a record of our guilt. We may claim innocence here and there; we may be better in some areas than others; we may have succeeded where others have failed – but the fact remains that we are 'guilty of all'.

The record of our guilt. That is the first thing the law discloses. But it discloses.

Secondly, the reality of God's grace. Now you may be asking 'Where is the grace of God in these verses?'. You may even feel with John Calvin that 'James seems more sparing in proclaiming the grace of Christ that it behoved an Apostle to be'! Well, I agree that although it is not stated explicitly here, it is suggested irresistibly. The section we have just studied ended with each one of us 'guilty of all'. We were in a position where we could cry with the Psalmist 'O Lord, enter not into judgement with Thy servant: for in Thy sight shall no man living be justified' (Psalm 143:3) and ask 'If You, Lord, should keep account and treat us according to our sins, O Lord, who could stand?' (Psalm 130:3 The Amplified Bible).

We need to be very clear in our thinking here, and to recognise our precise relationship to God in the matter of His law. As Christians we are under a most searching moral obligation to keep it in every part, yet at the same time we may dare to say this: that just as we were not saved by our obedience before our conversion, so we are not kept saved by our obedience after conversion. This is because the question of being saved, of being justified, *is not a matter of law at all*, but of grace, through faith. It is a matter, as Paul put it, of 'not having a righteousness of my own, which is based on law, but that which is through faith in Christ, the righteousness from God that depends on faith' (Philippians 3:9 RSV). As Paul also reminds us '. . . Christ is the end of the law for righteousness to every one that believeth' (Romans 10:4).

Here, surely, is truth that leads us to the wonder of God's grace! He does not lower the standards for us when we become Christians. He does not excuse our sins and failures, but in terms of our justification we are treated as being 'in Christ' (2 Corinthians 5:17), and we are 'accepted in the Beloved' (Ephesians 1:6). As far as justification is concerned, the penalty for every sin of every believer, from birth to death, has been paid once for all in the death of Christ, while the life of Christ, in all of its perfect obedience to the law, is the only life which God brings into His reckoning! Could there be anything more wonderful than that? As Samuel Davies once put it –

> *Great God of Wonders! all Thy ways*
> *Are matchless, godlike and divine;*
> *But countless acts of pardoning grace*
> *Beyond Thine other wonders shine.*
> *Who is a pardoning God like Thee?*
> *Or who has grace so rich and free?*

Chapter 5

THE CHRISTIAN AND GOD'S LAW – II

*'So speak ye, and so do, as they that shall be judged
by the law of liberty.*

*For he shall have judgement without mercy, that
hath shewed no mercy; and mercy rejoiceth against
judgement'.* (James 2:12-13)

This is the second of two studies over which we have put
the general heading 'The Christian and God's Law'. In the
previous passage (vv 8–11) He showed us that the Bible is
the royal law which convicts all of us as sinners. Even as
believers we are all guilty of breaking the law of God. Paul
says that 'all have sinned, and come short of the glory of
God' (Romans 3:23) and it is important to notice that that
second verb is in the present, continuous tense. All of us
have sinned *and are coming short* of the glory of God in our
daily life. Our best is short of the glory of God. Yet also,
by implication if not by statement, we saw God's wonderful grace in the justification of His believing people. Justification has put us into that position where all of our
disobedience – past, present and future – has been totally
debited to Christ's account and dealt with by Him at the
cross. Moreover, all of Christ's obedience to the law – that
obedience that enabled Him to say, 'I do always those
things that please Him (God)' (John 8:29); that obedience
that enabled Him to say to His fellow men, 'Which of you
convicts me of sin?' (John 8:46 RSV); that obedience that
enabled Him to say of the devil, 'He has no power over me'
(John 14:30 RSV) – all of that obedience is credited to the
individual believer. Even with all of its wonder forgiveness
is only a part of salvation. Salvation does not merely mean

that the moment a man comes to Christ everything that he
has done in the past has been forgiven and put out of the
way. That is only part of the truth. The other wonderful
thing is that from that moment onwards, regardless of
what that person is, God looks upon him in terms of his
eternal relationship as found in Christ.

> *Because my sinless Saviour died*
> *My guilty soul is counted free*
> *For God the Just is satisfied*
> *To look on Him and pardon me.*

That is the wonder of justification. But does that mean
that a Christian can behave carelessly in any way he
chooses? If it is true that all of his sin, past, present and
future, has been put out of the way in terms of justification,
then can he go ahead and live just as he pleases, without
danger? Theologically, that is called antinomianism'. In
practical terms it is lunacy. In biblical terms it is impossible. We are *not* free, as Christians, to do as we please. We
cannot afford to be careless, and James brings this in by
mentioning for the first time the issue of judgement to
come. In verse 12 he says that his readers 'shall be judged',
and twice in verse 13 he uses the word 'judgement'.

Three main headings will give us a clear picture of what
James is saying here.

1. *The reckoning we must face* – 'they that shall be judged
by the law of liberty' (v. 12).

James is saying two things here.

Firstly, he makes *a firm statement* – 'they shall be
judged'. The Bible does say for some people there will be
no condemnation (in Romans 8:1 for instance), but it does
not say that for anyone there will be no judgement.
Notice the distinction very clearly. In the parable about
believers and unbelievers described as sheep and goats,
Jesus began by saying 'When the Son of man shall come

in His glory, and all the angels with Him, then He will sit on His glorious throne. Before Him will be gathered *all the nations. . .*' (Matthew 25:31–32 RSV). Paul says that 'we shall *all* stand before the judgement-seat of Christ' (Romans 14:10) and that 'we must *all* appear before the judgement seat of Christ' (2 Corinthians 5:10). There is the firm scriptural statement, and there is a special word in it for two kinds of people.

(1) *There is a warning to the unbeliever who thinks that he will be excused.* Psalm 10 gives a devastating analysis of the unbeliever's thinking on this issue, and it seems to me to be all summed up in verse 11. This is the unbeliever thinking. This is the unregenerate man. 'God hath forgotten: he hideth his face; he will never see it.' Do you see the line of thinking? God has forgotten the past. He hides His face as to the present. He will never see it in the future. That is what the unbeliever hopes and thinks and at times even believes – that God has forgotten, that He is not looking at what is happening in the present and He is not going to see things in the future. Yet nothing could be further from the truth. Psychologist William James once said that every physical sensation and every contact a man has with the outside world leaves a permanent trace on a thousand million cells in the human brain. What a sobering thought! Everything that you say and do and think leaves its trace and mark on a thousand million cells in the human make-up. Down there in the nerve complexities and cells and fibres and molecules of the human chemistry, everything that you have said, been and done is recorded permanently – and will the God who made that recording instrument forget what is recorded? The Bible says 'God requireth that which is past' (Ecclesiastes 3:15). God is going to call it up. God is going to demand it from you. God is going to ask for a record. God is going to examine the books. God is going to require every thought that has

passed through your mind, every word that has passed your lips, every action that has occupied your body. God has not forgotten it. It is not just water under the bridge. It is recorded in the very fabric of your personality and it is recorded in the books that will be opened on the day of judgement. Here is the utter lunacy of the man who says, 'I am concerned that God is a Holy God. I am concerned that God is a God of judgement. I have a feeling that somehow the Bible might be right after all and I certainly know that I have sinned and have come short of the glory of God. I am determined to do better. I am going to live at a higher standard. I am going to be a better father. I am going to be a better son or daughter. I am going to be a better parent. I am going to be a better employee or employer. I am going to be more honest in my dealings, more moral in my associations. I am going to be better in the future!' Do you see the lunacy of it? God requires that which is past and no amount of resolution can alter that fact. God requires that which is past. But what about the present? 'God hides his face', says the unbeliever. 'God does not see what is going on. God knows nothing about it. I will just keep this to myself.' There are some who are living that kind of life in the secret place of the heart. There are things that pass through a man's mind, attitudes that occupy his heart, sins that he commits, and even his best friends know nothing whatever about them. What is more there is either the belief or at least a wistful longing in that perhaps God knows nothing about them either. But the Bible says that 'the Lord is a God of knowledge' (1 Samuel 2:3). You can go into the darkest room, walk on to the loneliest hillside, go into the bowels of the earth, ride to outer space, but there is nothing that you are, or say, or think, or do, that God does not know about. 'He that planted the ear, shall he not hear? He that formed the eye, shall He not see?' (Psalm 94:9).

And what of the future? – 'God will never see it' thinks the unbeliever. 'I just somehow have a feeling', he says 'that at the end of the day God will pass everything by and just forget about it.' So many millions of people are living with that vague and deadly philosophy that I believe we could make out a case for identifying the devil's favourite text in the Bible. I mean by that the one he uses more often than any other. And what do you think that might be? Something to do with the severity of God? Something to do with the law of God? Something to do with the details of life that God will one day examine? No – I believe that the devil's favourite text in the Bible might well be this – 'God is love' (1 John 4:8). I believe that there will be multiplied millions of people in the torment of hell because of their superficial understanding of those three magnificent words 'God is love'. God is love, so I can get away with it. God is love, so He will not examine my life in detail. God is love so He is bound to forgive me. God is love and could never punish anybody. God is love, so all this pressure to be converted, to be born again, is unnecessary.' And that kind of thing leads a man straight to hell *believing that God is love*.

Surely that underlines the importance of what James is saying here. He is giving a warning to the unbeliever who thinks he will be excused. He will *not* be excused. The moment is going to come when every unbeliever is going to stand in the presence of an all-knowing, all-wise, all-loving but all-holy God. Every single thought, word, deed and action that have occupied his life are going to rise up and stand between him and God – and one only of those will be sufficient to send him to a Christless and hopeless eternity. Perhaps I should make this even more personal at this point. If *you* are trying to harbour a thought that you will be excused, that God will see you all right in the end, on some vague and shallow basis, if you are clinging to a false understanding of those three marvellous words, 'God is love', then may the spirit of God speak to your heart and shake you free from that position, because you are trusting in that which is sand.

(2) *There is a warning to the believer who thinks he will not be examined.* Paul says that at the judgement everyone will 'receive good or evil, according to what he has done in the body' (2 Corinthians 5:10 RSV). While the believer's rejection is out of the question, the believer's reward is very much *in* question. God is going to sift every word, action and thought of the believer, not for the question of acceptance or rejection – that is over and done with for the believer – but for the question of his reward. The Bible says that every man's work 'will be revealed with fire, and the fire will test what sort of work each one has done. If the work which any man has built on the foundation survives, he will receive a reward. If any man's work is burned up, he will suffer loss, though he himself will be saved, but only as through fire' (1 Corinthians 3:13–15 RSV). We ought to note in passing that it is the *work* that will be tried by fire, and not the man. There is no support here for the doctrine of purgatory, which is not found anywhere in the Bible from beginning to end. Nevertheless, here is a warning to the believer whose understanding of justification and his relationship to God is so superficial that he thinks 'Everything will be marvellous, I am going to heaven and there is no judgement for me and I am not going to be examined, so I can just live exactly as I please. All my sin is gone and forgiven and for me there will be no kind of examination whatever!' That is not what the Bible says! It teaches that believers, too, are going to be examined. Every part of our work and life will come under God's all-knowing review. That is a firm statement – we 'shall be judged.'

Secondly, James shows that in the matter of judgement

there is a *final standard* – we shall be judged 'by the law of liberty'. It is not only true all men will stand before God, but all shall be judged righteously. When Abraham was pleading for the inhabitants of Sodom, he made, in the form of a question, a statement which is absolutely pivotal for our understanding of what is going to happen on the day of judgement. 'Shall not the Judge of all the earth do right?' (Genesis 18:25). Sometimes I am asked what happens at the judgement to little children who died in infancy, and the heathen who never heard the gospel at all, and those who had a limited opportunity to hear it. I think we could tie ourselves in knots trying to answer that kind of question in detail, and that it is always much safer to go just as far as the Bible goes and no further. Abraham said 'Shall not the Judge of all the earth do right?' That is the answer to the question – to the perplexed parent, to the concerned missionary, to the confused young Christian. 'Shall not the Judge of all the earth do right?' Yes, He will. There is a verse in Isaiah that is so little understood, almost never preached on, and yet one which marries right into this point, and it is this – 'He shall see of the travail of His soul, and shall be *satisfied*' (Isaiah 53:11). When the day of judgement has come and gone, when all the effect of all the preaching, in all the world, by every generation is over and done with, the Lord Jesus, in a magnificent and mysterious way 'shall see of the travail of His soul, and shall be satisfied'. We shall all be judged by one final standard and that is the revealed will of God to the individual. To some it has been the light of nature, to some the law of Moses, and to some the light of the gospel, yet every man will be judged by the same final standard.

Ultimately we are to be judged by the light of the glorious gospel of Jesus Christ. 'The law of liberty' is how James describes it. That seems a paradox – law and liberty seem to be opposite words. Yet at this precise point they come together in a wonderful way. There are three senses in which we can call the Bible the law of liberty as far as Christians are concerned–

(a) *We are free from the law's covenant*. It has been said that Paul and James teach different truths, that they are in opposition to one another. Yet the closer you examine their writings the more you will see that that is not true. In Romans 10 Paul's great burden and prayer is that 'Israel might be saved', and yet he sees them blinded by a terrible ignorance of the truth in such a way that as he puts it they are 'going about to establish their own righteousness' (Romans 10:3). What an expressive phrase! They were working at it, they were trying hard to satisfy God. All of their religion, with its rituals and ceremonies, was encrusted with that which they thought would contribute to their own salvation. They were 'going about to establish their own righteousness'. Now in theory, if a man kept the whole law of God from beginning to end, then he *would* be saved – but these Jews were turning a blind eye to all that God had said and done since those days, and they were still going about to save themselves by the works of the law. While they were doing so, Paul was preaching the magnificent liberating law of the gospel, which is that 'Christ is the end of the law for righteousness to everyone that believeth' (Romans 10:4). They were going about to establish their own righteousness, and had 'not submitted themselves unto the righteousness of God' (Romans 10:3). What a difference in the two phrases – they were 'going about', and they had not 'submitted themselves'. The Jews had missed the whole point of the gospel which is that Christ had fulfilled the law's conditions on behalf of all believers and with the coming of Christ there was a new covenant, a new law, the law of the gospel, the law of liberty. We are free from the law's covenant. Christ is the end of the law for righteousness to everyone who believes.

(b) *We are free from the law's curse.* In Bruce Hunt's book *For a Testimony* there is a wonderful illustration by way of contrast of the point I am making here. During the Second World War, Hunt was captured by the Japanese, taken to Manchuria, and tried on some trumped up charge or another. We break into the story as he is waiting for the verdict. The court made its decision and the verdict was read in Japanese and then interpreted into Korean, and it came across to Bruce Hunt like this – 'You are without crime'. Hunt asked 'Is this a suspended sentence'. 'No', said the guard, 'this is a suspended judgement. It means that they have not found you guilty and if for two years you do not get into trouble, then everything will be all right.' Hunt then asked why was it a suspended judgement? The guard explained that while the court had not found him guilty, neither had they declared him not guilty. The judgement one way or the other had been left hanging. If nothing came up within the next two years, then the case would be dropped. It now all depended on how the prisoner behaved. If he behaved well for a certain period of time, then the case would be dropped. But if during that period of time he should do something that offended the authorities, then all that he had done in the past would be brought up against him again.

Now that is an illustration by contrast. The believer is in a position where his liberty means much more than that. The Bible says 'Christ redeemed us from the curse of the law, having become a curse for us' (Galatians 3:13 RSV). The judgement and the penalty of God against our sin is not left hanging, it is not suspended in mid-air. It has been paid and executed by Christ on behalf of every single one of His people, and we are set free from the curse of the law which is condemnation. When we speak of being justified and made right with God, we are not saying that in the case of believers God has made an exception to His universal

law that the wages of sin is death. God has never made
one single exception to that universal law. The wages of
sin *is* death. Then how can it be that people whose lives
have been full of sin are set free? The answer is that for
all who believe in Christ, God has found a Substitute in
Whom that penalty and condemnation and judgement and
curse and separation and hell have been fully meted out.
In the majesty and the miracle of the cross we find the
wonderful biblical truth that God is both just and the
justifier of His believing people.

Charles Wesley put it in this way:

> *No condemnation now I dread;*
> *Jesus, and all in Him is mine!*
> *Alive in Him, my living Head,*
> *And clothed in righteousness divine,*
> *Bold I approach the eternal throne,*
> *And claim the crown, through Christ, my own.*

We are removed and freed from the curse of the law
because Jesus Christ was made a curse for us. His suffering
is my release. His death is my life. His hell is my heaven.
By His stripes we are healed. Praise God, we are free
from the curse of the law!

(c) *We are free from the law's compulsion.* To the unbeliever the law is an outward and external thing, pressing
against him, making demands upon him that he does not
want to fulfil. But in the new covenant, in the law of
liberty, all that has been changed. The Bible puts it like
this – 'Behold, the days are coming, says the Lord, when I
will make a new covenant with the house of Israel and the
house of Judah, not like the covenant which I made with
their fathers when I took them by the hand to bring them
out of the land of Egypt, my covenant which they broke,
though I was their husband, says the Lord. But this is
the covenant which I will make with the house of Israel

after those days, says the Lord: I will put my law within them, and I will write it upon their hearts: and I will be their God, and they shall be my people' (Jeremiah 31:31–33 RSV). Do you see the difference? To the unbeliever the law is an outward thing, pressing in upon them, making demands on him against their inclination, but God has put His law *within the heart* of the believer. For the Christian, obedience to the law of God is not a question of outward pressure, but of inward pleasure. The Psalmist says 'I delight to do thy will, O my God: yea, thy law is *within my heart*' (Psalm 40:8). If you are a Christian and feel in your inward heart a desire to do the will of God, then what you have is a God-given sense that you are free from the law's compulsion.

J. Stuart Holden. in his book *Chapter by Chapter through the Bible* says this – 'The law of liberty is the law of love. Christ makes men good, not by outward restraint but by inward restraint; not by inspired fear, but by infused passion. It is the glory and transcendence of the gospel that it creates an instinct of obedience in forgiven souls. We find complete enfranchisement in complete enslavement. His people are made free to do His will; and under its sway become too free to want to do any other.'

The Christian is not set free to do what *he* likes; he is set free to do what *God* likes. 'Those who are in the flesh cannot please God' (Romans 8:8 RSV), but the Christian has the potential to please God. We are free from the law's compulsion. Yet, it is a *law* of liberty. God has a sovereign right to exercise it and we have a subject's duty to obey it. Our response should be –

> *The Lord is King, I own His power,*
> *His right to rule each day and hour;*
> *I own His claim on heart and will,*
> *And His demands I would fulfil.*

2. *The responsibility we should feel* – 'So speak ye and so do' (v. 12).

In one sense the key word is the word 'ye' because James's earlier emphasis was on judging others. E. Stanley Jones tells of Indian students who once formed a 'Society for the confession of sins'. One of their members was asked 'Isn't it rather difficult meeting in a closed circle and confessing your sins to each other?' to which he replied 'But we don't confess our own sins, we confess other people's!' I have known some fellowships in the Christian church which could almost be called societies for the confession of other people's sins. May God forgive us for the spirit of criticism so prevalent amongst us in these days.

Having spoken so clearly about their judgement of other people, James says, 'So speak ye, and so do, as they that shall be judged by the law of liberty'. Are you a critic of other people? Then where do you stand? It has been said that the man who takes time to judge himself, will not have any time to take on any outside contracts! Remember the Bible's clear word that 'everyone of us shall give account of *himself* to God' (Romans 14:10). Some of us speak and behave as if we are going to have to give an account of everyone else in the church except ourselves!

Now notice the two areas James touches on –

(1) *Our words* – 'So speak ye'. James has already spoken about sins of the tongue in chapter 1 (vv 19 and 26) and most of chapter 3 deals with the same subject but the significant fact is surely this, that in considering the vast theme of the final judgement, he should specifically mention the use of the tongue. Speaking of God's judgements on his enemies, David says, 'So shall they make their own tongue to fall upon themselves' (Psalm 64:8). What a vivid picture! Here are people crushed out of the presence of God by sins of the tongue – criticism, slander, flattery,

lying, blasphemy, exaggeration, lightness and levity in holy things. Is it any wonder that Proverbs 18:21 says that 'death and life are in the power of the tongue'? And among believers, who can calculate the blessing and reward that would be ours were it not held back by our misuse of the tongue?

(2) *Our works* too – 'and so do'. In a phrase which could so well have been written by James himself, John says 'Little children, let us not love in word or speech but in deed and in truth' (1 John 3:18 RSV). Obedience should find its outlet in every part of our lives, and our obedience is the test of our love. Moreover, if we claim to be Christians, if we claim to have the law of God written in our hearts, then we should remember that one day we shall give an account of our stewardship. Responsibility brings accountability. An Anglican Bishop, in giving his final charge to candidates on the eve of their ordination used to say to them, 'Tomorrow I shall say to you, 'wilt thou ... ? Wilt thou ... ? Wilt thou ... ? But always remember that the day is coming when Another will say to you, 'Hast thou ... ? Hast thou ... ? Hast thou ... ? Responsibility brings accountability. The fact that God is going to take every word and action into account in the there and then means that we should take them into account in the here and now. That is the responsibility we should feel.

3. *The relationship we shall find* – 'For he shall have judgement without mercy, that hath showed no mercy; and mercy rejoiceth against judgement'. (v. 13).

The relationship we shall find on that day is the one between what we have been here and what will be done then. Paul speaks in Romans 11:22 of 'the goodness and severity of God' and we have both of them here, in the reverse order.

(1) *Here is the severity of God* – 'he shall have judgement without mercy, that hath showed no mercy'. No mercy

shown – no mercy given. That is severity, but it is not injustice. Earlier we saw that judgement was on the basis of revealed will, of nature, law and gospel. How has man responded to that revelation? To the revelation of nature – 'they changed the glory of the incorruptible God into an image' (Romans 1:23). To the light of the law? – 'For all have sinned and come short of the glory of God' (Romans 3:23). To the gospel? Jesus 'came unto His own, and His own received Him not' (John 1:11). The verdict is exactly the same, and 'the wrath of God is revealed from heaven against all ungodliness and unrighteousness of men' (Romans 1:18). Here is a man who has shown no mercy. He has been heartless, he has turned a blind eye to the needs of others, a deaf ear to the cries of the poor and the sick and the homeless and the refugees. His life has been centred on self. He is a man without love; a man without love for others is a man without grace; and a man without grace is a man who is lost. For him there is judgement without mercy. As someone has said, those whose hearts are not pierced by the Sword of God's Word shall certainly be cut down and destroyed by the axe of His judgement.

There is a word here for believers too. The believer who has withheld mercy from others will find that the mercy of greater reward will be withheld from him. This is the severity of God. Severity, but not injustice.

(2) *Here, too is the goodness of God* – 'and mercy rejoiceth against judgement', or as the RSV puts it, 'yet mercy triumphs over judgement'. We have already seen that we all deserve to be destroyed from God's presence. There is not one of us who can stand in the presence of God on our own merits. If a man's behaviour was the only issue that came in the matter of his acceptance before God, then who would be able to stand? In the light of a law which says 'For whosoever shall keep the whole law, and yet offend in one point, he is guilty of all' who would be

able to stand? Nobody. And yet mercy triumphs over judgement. God is going to bring into His eternal glory a multitude of men whom no man can number, those whose merciful lives marked by love and service show that they have laid hold on that greater mercy that God offers to sinners in Christ.

The mercy of God reflected in the life of the believer is going to triumph over judgement so that John can dare to say that 'we may have confidence for the day of judgement' (1 John 4:17 RSV). What a wonderful thought! Not brashness, not boasting, but boldness in the day of judgement. Not that our works of love and mercy are the *ground* of our confidence, but they are proofs of that greater mercy which will in turn be seen to triumph over the judgement that would otherwise overwhelm us.

When the saintly Puritan theologian Thomas Hooker was lying on his death bed in 1647 somebody said to him 'Brother, you are going to receive the reward of your labours', to which Hooker replied 'Brother, I am going to receive mercy'. God is a God of judgement, a God of infinite care, a God of great detail, a God of perfect knowledge, and yet His mercy triumphs over judgement. Praise Him for that! When we stand in His presence, what we shall receive is not earned reward for our labours, but mercy.

John Greenleaf Whittier put it like this–

> *I have but Thee my Father; let Thy Spirit*
> *Be with me then to comfort and uphold:*
> *No gate of pearl, no branch of palm I merit,*
> *Nor street of shining gold.*

> *Suffice it if – my good and ill unreckoned,*
> *And both forgiven through Thy abounding grace –*
> *I find myself by hands familiar beckoned*
> *Unto my fitting place.*

There, from the music round about me stealing,
I fain would learn the new and holy song,
And find at last, beneath Thy trees of healing
The life for which I long.

Chapter 6

FAITH AND WORKS – I

'What doth it profit, my brethren, though a man say he hath faith, and have not works? can faith save him?

If a brother or sister be naked, and destitute of daily food,

And one of you say unto them, Depart in peace, be ye warmed and filled; notwithstanding ye give them not those things which are needful to the body; what doth it profit?

Even so faith, if it hath not works, is dead, being alone.

Yea, a man may say, Thou hast faith, and I have works: shew me thy faith without thy works, and I will shew thee my faith by my works.

Thou believest that there is one God; thou doest well: the devils also believe, and tremble.'   (James 2:14–19)

The whole central thrust of the Epistle of James is crystallised in the passage we begin to study at this point. The theme of verses 14–26 is faith and works, and the whole Epistle is a series of variations on the theme. The passage we are now beginning to look at is probably one of the most misunderstood passages in the Bible, and perhaps at first glance it is not difficult to see why that is so. In verse 17 James says 'faith, if it hath not works, is dead, being alone', and in verse 20 he says 'wilt thou know, O vain man, that faith without works is dead?'. In verse 24 he insists that 'by works a man is justified, and not by faith only', and concludes in verse 26 'so faith without works is dead also'. Now that seems on the surface to run clean contrary to the biblical doctrine of justification by faith, and especially with Paul's insistence on that great truth. Paul says 'For we hold that a man is justified by faith apart from works of the law' (Romans 3:28 RSV); James says 'Ye see then how that by works a man is justified, and not by faith only'. But if Paul and James are in conflict then the whole of the New Testament is in ruins. The whole authority and unity of the Bible are at stake here. But *are* they in conflict? Of course it is possible to make them appear in conflict by quoting those two isolated texts out of context. But in that way one could take something that Jesus said and make it contradict something that Paul said. One could take Moses and Isaiah and make them contradictory too. It is even possible to take the consecutive works of one man and make them apparently contradict each other. A classic example is in Proverbs 26. 4–5 – 'Answer not a fool according to his folly, lest thou also be like unto him. Answer a fool according to his folly, lest he be wise in his own conceit.' But there is no contradiction in fact. The first statement says that we should not trade foolish arguments with a man, while the second says that we must give a wise answer, even to a fool to prevent him thinking that his folly is unanswerable.

Now to the so-called conflict between James and Paul. The best way to tackle it is to get down to a close examination of what James says here. Three things form the structure of this passage.

1. *There is a false claim* – 'What doth it profit my brethren, though a man say he hath faith, and have not works? can faith save him?

If a brother or sister be naked, and destitute of daily food,

And one of you say unto them, Depart in peace, be ye warmed and filled; notwithstanding ye give them not those things which are needful to the body; what doth it profit?' (vv 14–16)

'Thou believest that there is one God; thou doest well: the devils also believe, and tremble.' (v 19)

(1) *Notice what is made.* It is a claim – 'though a man *say* he hath faith, and have not works'. The whole passage hinges on that single word 'say'. It is a claim, not necessarily a fact. A man says 'I have faith; I am a Christian' – and James's reaction is 'Well, I would like to see evidence of your faith before I can accept your claim'.

James is not arguing whether or not faith saves a man, but whether a mere *profession* of faith is sufficient. A man says 'I am a Christian'; James says, 'Produce the evidence', and in taking that line he is being thoroughly biblical. Paul says 'Therefore if any man be in Christ, he is a new creature: old things are passed away; behold all things are become new' (2 Corinthians 5:17). The word 'behold' could be translated 'look for yourself'. A man should not have to give his testimony by word of mouth before it is obvious by the quality of his life that he is a changed man.

(2) *Notice what is missing* – 'What doth it profit my brethren'. This is the open challenge that James makes. Of what use is *that* kind of faith, a faith that can be summed up in words only? James found at least three things missing –

(a) *There was no communion with God* – 'Thou believest that there is one God; thou doest well: the devils also believe and tremble' (v. 19).

This man believed in one true God. Several modern translations, including The Amplified Bible, render the phrase 'I believe that God is One', and of course that was the beginning of the great Jewish statement of faith – 'Hear, O Israel: The Lord our God is one Lord' (Deuteronomy 6:4). This was the great distinguishing mark of the true Judaistic faith. When Paul speaks in 1 Corinthians 8 of false idols and of the sacrifices being offered to them, he adds most significantly, 'But to us there is but one God, the Father...' (1 Corinthians 8:6). And the man we are examining here says the same thing 'I believe that God is One'. This is his testimony, his statement of faith. Now notice James's two comments on that. First of all he says, 'thou doest well'. James was a gentleman, he was courteous. He said, 'You believe in one God; that is good'. James knew the man was not really converted (we are going to see that later), but he was prepared to commend good where he saw it. He did not reject the man out of hand. It would be a lovely thing if Christians learned to be courteous, to be gentlemen and gentle-women. It is one thing to know the scriptures – it is another thing to be gentlemanly, to be courteous and kind, to see the best in the worst.

But now notice James's second comment – 'the devils also believe and tremble', or as J. B. Phillips paraphrases it 'So you believe that there is one God? That's fine. So do all the devils in hell, and shudder in terror.' Is James right in saying that the devils 'Believe'? One only has to glance at the Gospels to see. At Gadara, the evil spirits in the two men cried out to Jesus 'What have you to do with us, O Son of God?' (Matthew 8:29 RSV). The man in the synagogue with an unclean spirit cried out 'What have you to do with us, Jesus of Nazareth? Have you come to destroy us? I know who you are, the Holy One of God' (Mark 1:24 RSV). At Galilee, we read that 'whenever the unclean spirits beheld him, they fell down before him and cried out, "You are the Son of God"' (Mark 3:11 RSV). Later a man with an unclean spirit shouted 'What have you to do with me, Jesus, Son of the Most High God?' (Mark 5:7 RSV). Finally, Luke tells us that when Jesus was performing miracles 'demons came out of many, crying, "You are the Son of God"' (Luke 4:41 RSV). Evil spirits 'believed'. They recognised the unity of the Godhead, the deity of Christ, and the certainty of judgement to come. There are no atheists in hell. Even the devils 'believe' – but it is not saving faith. If I read the Bible correctly, every single man and woman who has ever drawn breath upon the face of the earth will one day fall down and acknowledge that 'Jesus Christ is Lord to the glory of God and the Father' (Philippians 2:11) – but it will not be to their salvation. For many, it will be too late. Indeed, we can go further, and say that the devil himself, in terms of knowledge about God, is a being of great faith. He believes in the existence of God, the power of God, the love of God. The devil clearly believes in the incarnation, the virgin birth, the sinless life of Christ, the power of the cross, the resurrection of Jesus. The devil believes that Jesus is going to return to this earth once again. Surely nothing could more vividly prove that theology is no substitute for saving faith, and that growth in knowledge is no substitute for growth in grace.

But why can we say that this man had no communion with God? Because James goes on to say, 'the devils also believe *and tremble*'. The Amplified Bible says 'they shudder in terror and horror such as make a man's hair stand on end and contract the surface of his skin'! That is the result of the faith the evil spirits have. But is that saving faith? Is that what saving faith does to a man? When a man becomes a Christian, does he shudder in terror, does his hair stand on end, does the surface of his skin contract, is he terrified at the very thought of God? Certainly not! 'Therefore being justified by faith, we have *peace* with God through our Lord Jesus Christ' says Paul in Romans 5:1. Later he writes of 'Christ Jesus our Lord: in whom we have boldness and access with confidence by faith in him' (Galatians 3:11–12). The kind of faith of which James is speaking here, the kind of faith that goes no further than head knowledge, which is shared even by evil spirits, does not bring a man into communion with God. John Calvin has said that knowledge of God can no more connect a man with God than the sight of the sun can carry him to heaven.

(b) *There was no compassion for others* 'If a brother or
sister be naked, and destitute of daily food, and one of you
say unto them, Depart in peace, be ye warmed and filled;
notwithstanding ye give them not those things which are
needful to the body; what doth it profit?' (vv 15–16)

As usual, James puts his point in a picture. Notice first
that he speaks of 'a brother or sister', a fellow Christian.
We have a special obligation to our brothers and sisters in
Christ – 'As we have therefore opportunity, let us do good
unto all men, especially unto them who are of the house-
hold of faith' (Galatians 6:10). We have a responsibility to
do good to all men, regardless of what they believe – but we
have a particular responsibility to our fellow-believers. In
James's picture, another detail is added – the fellow-
believer is 'ill-clad and in lack of daily food' (RSV). And
the professing Christian's response – 'Go in peace, be
warmed and filled' (RSV). Just words! No wonder James
asks 'What does it profit?' Here is a hungry man, clothed
in rags, and a professing Christian, seeing his need, says
'Do keep warm and well-fed, won't you?' What does it
profit? Do words put food in the hungry man's stomach?
Do good wishes keep his back warm? No – and James's
point is that neither will a profession of faith with no good
works to back it up make a man right with God.

As Thomas Manton says, 'The poor will not thank you
for your good wishes, neither will God for saying you have
faith'!

The Bible is so pertinent on this – 'But if any one has the
world's goods and sees his brother in need, yet closes his
heart against him, how does God's love abide in him?'
(1 John 3:17 RSV). How can a man conceivably say that
the love of God dwells in him when he sees a brother in
need and deliberately does nothing whatever to alleviate
that need? Will that kind of faith save him? James is quite
clear as to the answer to that question. James is not saying

that any man with works is saved, but that a man without them is not.

Let me press home the importance the Bible places on down to earth love expressed in kindness and help to the needy. James himself insists that 'Pure religion and unde- filed before God and the Father is this, To visit the father- less and widows in their affliction, and to keep himself unspotted from the world' (James 1:27). It is possible to be so concerned with evangelism, that we think of it as the only thing that qualifies as Christian service. Jesus was concerned with bodies and minds as well as with souls. He asks us to be concerned about people *as people;* our commission is the whole gospel for the whole man throughout the whole world.

Let no Christian avoid the impact of this. Can you make the kind of statement that that astonishing man Job once made – 'If I have withheld anything that the poor desired, or have caused the eyes of the widow to fail, or have eaten my morsel alone, and the fatherless has not eaten of it (for from his youth I reared him as a father, and from his mother's womb I guided him); if I have seen any one perish for lack of clothing, or a poor man without covering; if his loins have not blessed me, and if he was not warmed with the fleece of my sheep; if I have raised my hand against the fatherless, because I saw help in the gate; then let my shoulder blade fall from my shoulder and let my arm be broken from its socket' (Job 31:16–22 RSV). Can you make that kind of statement? What a challenge to our heartless orthodoxy! – and what a contrast to the man in James's illustration, a man with no compassion for others.

(c) *There was no conversion of self* – 'can faith save him?', or, as The Amplified Bible puts it, 'Can such faith save his soul?' By giving no answer, James means that the answer is 'No'! Let me emphasise again that James is *not* saying that a man is not saved by grace and through faith. What he is asking is whether just any kind of faith will do. Will this man's faith do – the kind of faith that says, 'I believe, I am converted, I have become a Christian, I have joined a church' – if he has no works of love to back it up? There is a vivid illustration of the answer in the story of Simon the sorcerer in Samaria. He was an amazing man in many ways. People even called him 'the great power of God' (Acts 8:10). Then Philip came and preached in Samaria, as a result of which 'Simon himself believed also; and ... was baptised' (v. 13). Later on, Peter and John came to Samaria and the Holy Spirit began to be manifested through their ministry. When Simon saw what was happening 'he offered them money saying, "Give me also this power, that on whosoever I lay hands, he may receive the Holy Ghost" ' (vv 18–19). Peter's reply was direct and devastating – 'Your silver perish with you, because you thought you could obtain the gift of God with money! You have neither part nor lot in this matter, for your heart is not right before God... you are in the gall of bitterness and in the bond of iniquity' (vv 20, 21 and 23 RSV). This man 'believed', he was baptised, but he was in the bondage of sin, clearly an unconverted man. Simon's life was still dominated by the capital 'I' whereas a Christian's testimony is 'I am crucified with Christ' (Galatians 2:20).

Do you claim to have faith? Do you say that you are a Christian? Then do you have communion with God? Do you have peace with God, or are you having a running battle with Him all the time? Do you have compassion for others, real love and concern? Are you truly converted? Are you crucified with Christ? Are you a changed person living a new life? That is the impact of what James is saying.

2. *There is a foolish compromise* – 'Yea, a man may say, Thou hast faith, and I have works: shew me thy faith without thy works, and I will shew thee my faith by my

works' (v. 18).

There are many different interpretations of this verse, and if we accept that some kind of dialogue is going on here, the problem hinges on the placing of the quotation marks. The truth must obviously fit in with the general drift of the whole passage and I think we can find a happy interpretation in those terms. Let us divide the verse into two. First of all there is *the argument*, and then there is *the answer*.

(1) Here is *the argument* – 'Yea, a man may say "Thou hast faith and I have works" '. This is a snatch of conversation between two people. One is speaking to the other about the gospel, about the necessity of coming to Christ. His friend seeking perhaps to blur the edge of the issue says, 'Well, you see, I am a practical Christian. My religion is, "Do as you would be done by". I believe in trying to live up to the Commandments, the golden rule, the Sermon on the Mount. On the other hand, you have so much more faith, you are rather more concerned with doctrine and theology than I am. But there is no need for us to have an argument. Surely we are both right. *You have faith – I have works.* We are just different kinds of Christians, that is all. We are both the children of God. Don't you try to convert me to your way of thinking and I won't try to convert you to mine. There is room for both of us in the world. You are a sort of theological, doctrinal Christian concentrating on faith and belief and so on, and I am a practical Christian. Your Christianity is believing, my Christianity is doing.'

That is the argument, and it is still alive today. People say that what we need is a practical and pragmatic Christianity. All these doctrinal issues of the virgin birth, the incarnation, Christ's substitutionary death, conversion, sanctification and so on are irrelevant. People are dying and starving in the world. Let us go out and help them, following the example of Jesus, and then we will be received by God on the basis of our good works. But these people are tragically wrong. They have substituted service for salvation, and compassion for conversion. But that is a foolish compromise. Humanitarianism can never make a man right with God. A Buddhist, a humanist, an atheist, can have a concern for his fellow men. There are men and women literally laying down their lives in sacrificial service, in meeting the needs of those who are in desperate need, physically and mentally, and who do not even believe in the existence of God. The argument is clearly false.

(2) *Here is the answer.* 'Shew me thy faith *without* thy works, and I will shew thee my faith *by* my works.'

Here is the Christian's answer to his confused friend's false argument. 'Show me faith without works (if you can! – after all, faith is invisible). As for me, I will demonstrate the reality of my faith by my works.' This is the consistent biblical position. It is not good enough to have your name on a card, a baptismal roll, a church register. If there is no fruit of the Holy Spirit in your life your testimony is false. Jesus said, 'By their fruits ye shall know them' (Matthew 7:20). James says plainly 'I will show you my faith *by* my works'. He does not say it boastfully, but gratefully. He says, 'If my faith is called into question by men or the devil, then praise God I can point to a changed life, and my life bears out the validity of my claim'.

Two men were arguing over this very point of faith and works while they were being rowed across a river. The oarsman was a Christian, and asked whether he could join in the discussion. Given permission, he said 'Let us assume that one of these oars is faith and the other one is works. We'll take the "works" oar out of the water and just use "faith".' As a result, of course, the boat went around in circles. After a while he said, 'Perhaps we have got the wrong one. We'll put the "faith" oar in the boat and just use "works".' The result, of course, was the same. They still went around in circles. Finally, he put both oars in together, and pulled straight for the shore. His point was made!

In a real Christian there is faith *and* works. True Christian experience is that a man is saved *by* grace, *through* faith, *unto* good works, and in that way faith and works blend together.

We can now look at the remaining phrase, in which James expresses.

3. *A firm conviction* – 'Even so faith, if it hath not works, is dead, being alone' (v. 17).

James refused to be shaken from this point. It runs through the whole passage, but it is vitally important to notice that James does not say, 'faith is dead without works' – that is, until works are added. It is not the addition of works that brings faith into life. What James says, is that if people claim to have faith and yet have no good works, then that faith is not saving faith. It is not 'faith working through love' (Galatians 5:6 RSV). And far from contradicting Paul, James is confirming his teaching. It is true that Paul said 'a man is justified by faith apart from works of law' (Romans 3:28 RSV); but he also spoke of those who 'profess to know God, but they deny Him by their deeds . . .' (Titus 1:16 RSV).

Paul's great theme is that nobody can procure salvation by the works of the law. James's great theme is, nobody can prove their salvation except by works of love. There is no disagreement there. Paul and James are warning different people and making a different point. This line of thought is developed in the next study. For the moment, our concern should be to examine our hearts on the issues involved, and to pray that we might 'lead a life worthy of the Lord, fully pleasing to Him, bearing fruit in every good work and increasing in the knowledge of God' (Colossians 1:10 RSV).

Chapter 7

FAITH AND WORKS – II

'But wilt thou know, O vain man, that faith without works is dead?

Was not Abraham our father justified by works, when he had offered Isaac his son upon the altar?

Seest thou how faith wrought with his works, and by works was faith made perfect?

And the scripture was fulfilled which saith, Abraham believed God, and it was imputed unto him for righteousness: and he was called the Friend of God.

Ye see then how that by works a man is justified, and not by faith only.

Likewise also was not Rahab the harlot justified by works, when she had received the messengers, and had sent them out another way?

For as the body without the spirit is dead, so faith without works is dead also.' (James 2:20–26)

In these verses, James concludes his central statement of the theme of the whole Epistle. Before we begin to examine it in detail, we need to remember that he is not challenging the man who claims to be saved *because* of his works, but the man who claims to be saved in spite of the fact that he has no good works to back up his claim.

Notice the three ways in which James deals with the subject.

1. *How he introduces it* – 'But wilt thou know, O vain man'. (v. 20). The Amplified Bible puts it perfectly – 'Are you willing to be shown proof . . . ?' What a most incisive question! Some people ask questions about the Christian

faith because they want to believe, but others ask questions because they want to disbelieve. James is challenging this kind of superficial questioning, and we should do the same.

Jesus put the points clearly – 'And this is the judgement, that the light has come into the world, and men loved darkness rather than light, because their deeds were evil. For every one who does evil hates the light, and does not come to the light, lest his deeds should be exposed' (John 3:19–20 RSV). Men are not *willing* to know the truth, they are not *willing* to understand, they are not *willing* to accept Christ – and the reason is that they prefer their sin. This challenge needs to be pressed home to the unconverted.

But there is a challenge to Christians too. Are *we* willing to know the Word of God? Are we willing to understand what God is saying to us in the pages of His Word? And are we willing to obey whatever God commands?

Then notice the phrase '*O vain man*'. The word 'vain' is the Greek word 'kenos', which means 'empty' – in this case, empty of spiritual understanding. Let us be clear on this – noise and knowledge do not necessarily go together. A man may be full of eloquent argument, but without the enlightening of the Holy Spirit he remains in spiritual darkness. Without the leading of the Holy Spirit, no man can find his way to the truth. Until he is given what James calls 'the wisdom that is from above' (James 3:17), then all of his knowledge is emptiness. When Peter made that great confession at Caesarea Philippi, 'You are the Christ, the Son of the Living God', Jesus told him 'Blessed are you Simon Bar-jona! For flesh and blood has not revealed this to you, but my Father who is in heaven' (Matthew 16:16–17 RSV); while Paul insists that 'the unspiritual man does not receive the gifts of the Spirit of God, for they are folly to him, and he is not able to understand them because they are spiritually discerned' (1 Corinthians 2:14 RSV). As Christians too, we need the Spirit of God before we can ever understand the Scriptures. It does not matter how long you have been a Christian, how mature you are, what your knowledge is, or how many texts you can quote off by heart, unless the Spirit of God directs your reading, enables your understanding and energises your will, the Bible will be of no spiritual value to you. We need to come to the Word of God with a sense of utter dependence upon the Holy Spirit to break open to us even the simplest of truths. 'But wilt thou know, O vain man?' asks James. That is how he introduces his subject. And to this vain and empty man James brings the authority, evidence and power of the Word of God.

2. *How he illustrates it.* In his illustration which takes in verses 21–25, James uses two heroes from the Old Testament hall of fame in Hebrews 11 – Abraham and Rahab. One was a man, one a woman; one a Jew, one a Gentile; one a patriarch, the other a prostitute. Perhaps he does this to show that the rule is the same for all. No fruit in the life is a sign of no root in the heart.

(1) *Abraham the patriarch* – 'Was not Abraham our father justified by works, when he had offered Isaac his son upon the altar?

Seest thou how faith wrought with his works, and by works was faith made perfect?

And the scripture was fulfilled which saith, Abraham believed God, and it was imputed unto him for righteousness: and he was called the Friend of God.

Ye see then how that by works a man is justified, and not by faith only' (vv 21–24).

The whole passage teems with truth. Notice first of all that James speaks of 'Abraham our father'. Physically he was the father of the nation, but spiritually he is the father of all who as Christians belong to the new Israel. Paul says ' . . . it is men of faith who are the sons of Abraham' (Galatians 3:7 RSV). James then goes on to say that

Abraham was 'justified by works'. Here is the crunch of the whole argument. James obviously does not mean that Abraham's justification, his standing with God, was the result of his works (his willingness to offer Isaac). In fact, James says very clearly, 'Abraham believed God, and it was imputed unto him for righteousness' (v. 23). Abraham was saved by faith – it was his faith that was counted unto him for righteousness. The work of sacrificing Isaac (or, rather, his willingness to sacrifice him) was not the *means* of Abraham's justification, nor was it the *moment* of justification. It was the *mark* of his justification. As the Amplified Bible puts it – 'Was not our father Abraham *shown* to be justified ... *by* his works ...'. In the words of Matthew Poole, 'Abraham's justification was not the absolution of a sinner, but the approbation of a believer'. It was the proof, the evidence, the sign, the seal of the fact that he had already believed God. That believing had been accounted and imputed unto him for righteousness, and as a sign that he really did believe God, he was prepared to offer his son Isaac. In Genesis 15 Abraham *said* that he believed God. In Genesis 22 he *showed* that he believed.

Now remember that James is still exposing the man who *claims* to be a Christian, but has no proof of his conversion. His argument is that a man must prove the reality of his faith. Abraham did, and James says 'Ye see then how that by works a man is justified, and not by faith only' (v. 24). The more I studied verses 22–23, the more I became convinced that, far from being an exaltation of works, they are an exaltation of faith! Notice there are four things, all linked with the word 'and' – 'Seest thou how faith wrought with his works, AND by works was faith made perfect? AND the scripture was fulfilled which saith, Abraham believed God, and it was imputed unto him for righteousness: AND he was called the Friend of God'. Let us examine these four in turn –

(a) *Faith's principle*. 'Faith wrought with his works'. Not, will you notice, 'works wrought with his faith'. The priority is given to faith because it was faith which led to the works. The work of obedience on Mount Moriah was a work of faith, as we are told in Hebrews 11:17 – 'By faith Abraham, when he was tested, offered up Isaac . . . ' It was his unshakeable faith in God that enabled him to take that step of naked obedience that seemed certain to shatter all his hopes. God had promised that his seed would be as the stars of the sky for number. He had this one son, Isaac. And God had apparently told him to take that son and slay him upon the altar! Yet such was the faith of this man Abraham that with all of his hopes held in the body of that precious son, he was prepared to see him slain, and to trust God with the consequencies. 'Faith wrought with his works', or, as the New English Bible puts it, 'Surely you can see that faith was at work in his actions?' James is not saying that faith plus works equals a Christian, but that true faith always produces works. This is the principle of faith. Faith is alive and active, and it works out from a believing heart into an obedient life.

(b) *Faith's proof*. '*And* by works was faith made perfect.' The truth here hinges on the word 'perfect'. It obviously does not mean that faith was insufficient until works were added. The explanation is illustrated in the use of the identical word in 2 Corinthians 12:9 where the Lord says to Paul – 'My grace is sufficient for thee: for my strength is made perfect in weakness'. God's strength was obviously not brought into being by Paul's weakness, or improved by it. What happened was that God's strength was *revealed* in Paul's weakness. The weaker Paul was, the more obvious it became that the grace of God was the secret of his power. There are countless millions of stars in the sky, and they are there all the time, but while the sun is shining and the sky is blue you cannot see a single one of them. But let the dusk, deepen into darkness and all the stars come into view. The greater the darkness, the clearer the stars will shine. And the greater man's weakness, the clearer the grace of God will shine through. Some of the greatest men of God, some of them whose spirituality has challenged me most of all, have not been strong, healthy, immensely talented men at all. They have been weak, diseased, crippled, humbled men in whom the grace of God has shone out like a million stars on a dark night.

'By works was faith made perfect?' His faith was shown to be real by his works. There were other tests and examples in Abraham's life, but surely this was the supreme one. As the New English Bible puts it, 'by these actions the integrity of his faith was fully proved'. When a man is prepared to take his only son and to slay him upon an altar when he already has a promise that he is going to be the father of a multitude like the sand on the seashore, and as the stars in the sky for number, then that is an illustration that the man's faith is real!

(c) *Faith's promise.* '*And* the scripture was fulfilled which saith, Abraham believed God and it was imputed unto him for righteousness.'

It was 30 years before that incident on Mount Moriah that God met Abraham and told him that he would have a son and eventually be the father of a multitude as the stars for number. Abraham's response was one of the greatest statements in the Old Testament – 'And he believed in the Lord; and he counted it to him for righteousness' (Genesis 15:6). This is the truth in which the Apostle Paul rejoices so greatly – 'Abraham believed God and it was counted unto him for righteousness' (Romans 4:3) – and when James speaks about him offering Isaac, he does not ignore Genesis 15:6, or disagree with it, he quotes it, and says 'the scripture was fulfilled'. The word 'fulfilled' is not a word about development, it is a word about demonstration. It is

also important for us to notice that the word 'righteousness' has the same root as the word 'justification'.
Abraham was justified 30 years before he offered Isaac on
Mount Moriah, and James agrees with this. The offering of
Isaac did not alter his justification, it did not strengthen his
justification, it did not improve his justification, it did not
add to his justification, it did not contribute to his justification, because none of these things can ever be done. Justification is a full, complete, entire, perfect, unalterable and
once for all judicial act of the grace of God in the heart of
man, and is laid hold of through faith alone in the person
and the work of the Lord Jesus Christ. Here is faith's
promise, that when a man turns to Christ in faith and
trusts Him as Saviour, he is justified in the sight of God,
not partially, but completely; not possibly, but certainly;
not temporarily but permanently. Justification has to do
not only with the forgiveness of a man's sins that are past,
but with the putting away once and for all time of every
single sin and blemish in that man's life, past and present
and future, that could ever stand between him and the
certainty of being glorified in the presence of God for ever.
In Charles Wesley's words:

> *No condemnation now I dread;*
> *Jesus, and all in Him, is mine.*
> *Alive in Him, my living Head,*
> *And clothed in righteousness divine*
> *Bold I approach the eternal throne,*
> *And claim the crown, through Christ my own.*

'He that heareth my word', said Jesus, 'and believeth on
Him that sent me, hath everlasting life, and shall not come
into condemnation: but is passed from death unto life'
(John 5:24). That is faith's promise.

(d) *Faith's privilege.* '*And* he was called the Friend of
God.' This title is borne out elsewhere in the Bible:

Jehoshaphat speaks to God of 'Abraham thy friend' (2 Chronicles 20:7), and God also refers to 'Abraham my friend' (Isaiah 41:8). What a wonderful statement that is! Faith introduces the sinner to the Saviour, and gives him the privilege of being God's friend! And this is not only for the Abrahams of this world, for people who give such a dramatic demonstration of their faith. Jesus told His disciples, 'I have called you friends' (John 15:15). Our thinking on this is usually the other way round. We have hymns beginning 'What a Friend we have in Jesus', and 'Thou art the sinners Friend'. But the emphasis here is that we are *His* friends! Immediately after the words quoted in John 15, Jesus said, 'for all things that I have heard of my Father I have made known unto you' (John 15:15). The Christian is given a dimension of understanding and knowledge of spiritual truth that is given to nobody else. What a wonderful privilege that we can share our secrets with God; it is even more wonderful that He should be willing to share His secrets with us! He *is* our Friend, of course, and we can share all our problems, needs and difficulties with Him; but we are also *His* friends. He shares with us that which He does not share with anyone else in the world.

When you come to the Bible, and God speaks to you through it, it is because you are His friend. He has told you a secret that He does not tell everybody. This is just a glimpse of the outworking of this glorious truth.

So much for Abraham the patriarch. Now we have:

(2) *Rahab the prostitute* – 'Likewise also was not Rahab the harlot justified by works, when she had received the messengers, and had sent them out another way?' (v. 25).

Why her story? We are not told, but these things seem to me to be relevant.

(a) *Her condition was so sinful.* She is described as 'the harlot'. There might have been a possible objection to

James's argument so far. People might have said, 'We can hardly be expected to compare with Abraham. Look at his background, and God's special dealings with him, and the promises that were made to him. We are just ordinary people. We are weak and tempted and so conscious of our sin. It is no good giving us the example of a great man like Abraham. He is so far removed from us to begin with, that somehow we just do not identify with him at all.' James's answer is to go right to the bottom of the social barrel, and alongside a patriarch, to quote a prostitute – to show that even from the least and lowest, from the youngest in the faith, from those with the deepest scars of their past life upon them, *God insists on works as evidence of faith*. There is a demand in the gospel *regardless of who you are*. But the wonderful thing is that it is a reasonable demand, because with every demand that God makes there comes the dynamic of the Holy Spirit to meet it – ' . . . His divine power hath given unto us all things that pertain unto life and godliness, through the knowledge of him that hath called us to glory and virtue' (2 Peter 1:3). Nobody can plead background, environment or anything else as an excuse for not displaying the fruit of the Spirit in their life. Rahab, after all, was a prostitute. Her condition was so sinful.

(b) *Her confession was so similar*. Rahab had become a believer. We are not told how, or when, but her confession of faith is in Joshua 2:11 – ' . . . the Lord your God, He is God in heaven above and in earth beneath'. How similar to the confession James quotes earlier in this chapter – 'There is one God'. The argument may be this. 'You know that Rahab was a believer, and in fact her confession of faith is very similar to yours. But was it her confession that proved she was saved? No, it was not. If all we had was a confession of faith from Rahab she would never have appeared in the heroes of faith in Hebrews 11. She made a confession of faith.

(c) *Her confirmation was so simple.* The confirmation of her faith was not easy, but simple, plain, clearcut. She not only *said* that she believed, she *showed* it. – 'By faith the harlot Rahab perished not with them that believed not, when she had received the spies with peace' (Hebrews 11:31). The confirmation of her faith was so simple. She received the spies in peace. She was prepared to be identified with the people of God. There were works in her life that proved that her confession of faith was no mere idle word. She put her own life in jeopardy in order to save the lives of two fellow believers. A woman who had ruined her life with lust at its lowest, now revealed her faith by love at its highest. The grace of God in that woman's life, not only forgave her, but transformed her, and the confession of her faith was made strikingly clear by her daring act of love and loyalty to the people of God in their great need.

James has introduced his point, and illustrated it. Now notice

3. *How he insists on it* – 'For as the body without the spirit is dead, so faith without works is dead also' (v. 26).

The truth that James has hammered out in verse 17 and again in verse 20, he underlines here with yet another picture. Generations of commentators have wrestled with the difficulties of getting to James's precise meaning here, yet a simple illustration can take us to the heart of it. If you were to discover somebody lying on the ground and did not know if he was alive or dead, you would hold a mirror to his face. If marks appeared on the mirror you would know that the body was alive, but if the mirror registered nothing whatever then you would know that the body was dead. James's picture is of a person claiming to be a Christian, to be alive in Christ. James takes the mirror of the Word of God and he places it alongside this person and then looks to see if anything registers. If something appears, then the claim is real, the body is alive. If nothing appears, it is dead. In His original creation God joined body and spirit together. In the new creation God joins faith and works together and what God has joined, we dare not put asunder.

Here is James's unflinching challenge, that probes and penetrates, and demands a response. And a glad and happy response is possible, for 'God is able to make all grace abound toward you; that ye, always having all sufficiency in all things, may abound to every good work' (2 Corinthians 9:8).

Chapter 8

THE SANITY OF HUMBLE SERVICE

'My brethren, be not many masters, knowing that we shall receive the greater condemnation. For in many things we offend all.' (James 3:1–2a)

James's style sometimes makes it difficult to know where one section ends and the next begins. Although it may seem rather arbitrary, a case can be made for making a break, or at least a pause, after the first sentence in verse 2, as I have done here. To begin with, James gives:

1. *A pointed instruction* – 'My brethren, be not many masters'.

The instruction is definite and precise, but of course its real meaning hinges on the word 'masters'. Some years ago, a friend of mine was contemplating school teaching as a career. He felt fairly clear that this was God's will for him, but at the very time when he was at the point of needing to be clear of the Lord's guidance he happened to read this particular verse in the J. B. Phillips version. Imagine how he felt, in the valley of decision, when he read, 'don't aim at adding to the number of teachers'! The RSV might have produced the same reaction as it says 'let not many of you become teachers', and we cannot escape the fact that the original word used here for 'masters' does come from the verb 'to teach', so that the root meaning is certainly there. This particular word 'masters' is used many times in the Bible. Jesus was addressed many times as 'Master'. He asked Nicodemus 'Art thou a *master* of Israel and knowest not these things'? (John 3:10). Again, when Joseph and Mary found the boy Jesus sitting in the temple in Jerusalem 'in the midst of the doctors' (Luke 2:46) and the word 'doctors' in our Authorised Version is, in the original Greek, exactly the same word 'masters' that we have here in James. So there are perhaps three interpretations with a claim of being the right one of this particular word.

The first is a special class of people within the Christian church. I have in mind, for instance, what it says in 1 Corinthians 12:28 – 'And God hath set some in the church, first apostles, secondly prophets, thirdly *teachers* . . . ', and in Ephesians 4:11 – 'And He gave some, apostles; and some prophets; and some, evangelists; and some, pastors and *teachers* . . . '. This may be what James means, a special technical office within the Christian church that is given in the Bible the name of 'teacher'.

Secondly, it might be any ministry of leading, teaching, or expounding the scriptures, or preaching the Word of God within the Christian church.

Thirdly, and very differently, there is the line John Calvin took in understanding the word as meaning 'self-constituted censors and reprovers of others'. If this is the right interpretation, then this is James's way of putting Jesus's instruction 'Judge not, that ye be not judged' (Matthew 7:1).

We can give space to all three of the possibilities outlined, by seeing here two warnings that James may be giving.

(1) *A warning against carnal ambition.* The office of teacher in the Christian church filtered through from the office of Rabbi in the Jewish church. The Rabbi was held in such an exalted position that if a man's father and a man's rabbi were captured by his enemies and one man could be ransomed, the man would be duty bound to ransom his rabbi and leave his father in captivity. When he was greeted in the streets, he would be fawned upon and

treated with tremendous deference. The very word 'rabbi' meant 'my great one'. This fawning and flattery, as we can imagine was more than flesh and blood could stand, which explains something very significant that Jesus said in Matthew 23:5–7 – 'But all their works they do for to be seen of men: they make broad their phylacteries, and enlarge the borders of their garments, and love the uppermost rooms at feasts, and the chief seats in the synagogues, and greetings in the markets, and to be called of men, Rabbi, Rabbi'. Now the teacher in the Christian church, although occupying a slightly different position, nevertheless seems potentially to have inherited some of the exalted status of the rabbi in the Jewish church – and with the status, the danger! People began to seek to be teachers because it put them above their fellowmen. It is in that context that Paul's word to Timothy immediately springs to mind. Paul spoke of those 'desiring to be teachers of the law, without understanding either what they are saying or the things about which they make assertions' (1 Timothy 1:7 RSV). In spite of their ignorance, their spiritual immaturity, they wanted to be teachers – carnal ambition! In the New Bible Commentary on this particular section, Andrew McNab says 'There seems to have been an eagerness on the part of many to speak in public, and a failure to recognise that the *fundamental qualification is learning*'. Mark that! When you cease to be a learner you cease to have any usefulness as a teacher. What a word for today! There are two edges to this particular sword, two things we must avoid.

Firstly, *indolence*. It is not 'be not *any* teachers'. James is not saying that no man should apply himself to studying the Word of God and communicating to others. There is a tremendous need in the Christian church today for sound teachers of the Word. On my first visit to America, a pastor said to me, 'We are suffering for what happened in this country 10 or 15 years ago when anybody with a bright tie, a big Bible and a flashy pair of socks was an evangelist'. In Britain, too, we have a surplus of the superficial and a dearth of depth in the ministry of the Word of God. There is a great need for teachers, for those who will give themselves to prayer and the ministry of teaching others. Indolence is a sin and we have a duty always to be praying Paul's prayer – 'Lord, what wilt Thou have me to do?' (Acts 9:6) and to obey his commands, 'Do not neglect the gift you have' (1 Timothy 4:14 RSV), and 'rekindle the gift of God that is within you' (2 Timothy 1:6 RSV). Whatever your position in the church, take that to heart! You *have* a gift, and you have a duty not to neglect it and to stir it up. Pray that the Holy Spirit will energise that which He has given you and will use you to God's glory and to the blessing of other people! We must avoid indolence. But we must also avoid –

Secondly, *insolence*. This may be the main thrust here. Do not be carnally ambitious. What a terrible amount of striving and wriggling and scheming there is in the Christian church today – to be chairman of this, secretary of that, leader of the other. If there is one thing worse than social climbing in the world, it is ecclesiastical climbing in the church. It is a loathsome thing. It grieves the Holy Spirit of God. It reminds one of Diotrephes, of whom John wrote that he 'loveth to have the pre-eminence' (3 John 9). Thomas Brooks once said 'Ambition is a gilded misery, a secret poison, a hidden plague, the engineer of deceit, the mother of hypocrisy, the parent of envy, the original of vices, the moth of holiness, the blinder of hearts, turning medicines into maladies and remedies into diseases. High seats are never but uneasy and crowns are always stuffed with thorns!'

The shortest chapter in Jeremiah is written mainly to one man. It is a very brief chapter, with only five verses in it, written to a man called Baruch, who seems to have been

Jeremiah's private secretary. At the time, Jeremiah was commanded by God to prophecy very hard things to his people, but Baruch wasn't prepared to settle down under that sort of thing. He was doing all that he could to find an easier time than the Lord was prophesying, or possibly for the opportunity to influence Jeremiah in what he was writing. And the Lord sent a message exclusively to this man Baruch, a message that comes across the centuries in one single, shattering sentence – 'And seekest thou great things for thyself, seek them not' (Jeremiah 45:5). Do you seek great things? Fine! – seek them for the Kingdom of God; seek them for the Lord Jesus; seek them for the sake of the Holy Spirit; seek them for the sake of the lost; seek them for the sake of God's people, but 'seekest thou great things for thyself – seek them not'. Here is a warning against carnal ambition.

(2) *There may well be a word here against a critical attitude.* Here is a word to those in a position of leadership. Leadership, even if it is God-given is no sign of superiority. No position in the Christian church is a reward, something we have earned. Men might heap their praises upon us, they might give us degrees and add titles to our names, but from God's point of view I am sure it is not a reward, it is not promotion, it is not a question of superiority. It is interesting that at this very point one of only a handful of men in the whole of history who will be able to claim to have been an apostle, adopts the phrase, 'my brethren'. Surely it is significant that at this very point James steps aside from his God-given position of apostleship and writes as an equal – 'my brethren'. Thomas Manton once wrote 'Proud nature thinketh itself somebody when it can get in to a chair of arrogance and cast out censures according to its own will and pleasure, as if God had advanced us into some higher rank and sphere, and all the world had been made to be our scholars'. Do you see the danger?

Self-assumed superiority soon leads to a critical attitude of others. There are two biblical antidotes to that sort of thing:

(a) *Remember the Master.* Whatever your position in the Lord's vineyard, remember that there is only One who is the Lord of the vineyard, and the Master of the harvest. Jesus said 'The servant is not greater than his Lord' (John 15:20). Can you afford to be proud, arrogant, critical and superior when you remember the Master, the One who said He came 'not to be ministered unto but to minister' (Mark 10:45)? Dare you be critical and high minded when you remember the Master?

(b) *Remember the ministry.* Teaching, leading, preaching, being chairman of this and president of that are ministries, and the root meaning of 'ministry' is 'to serve'. To be a servant of others, not the promoter of self. That is why Peter writes to church elders 'Tend the flock of God that is your charge . . . not as domineering over those in your charge, but being examples to the flock' (1 Peter 5:2–3 RSV). This does not mean a spineless sort of approach to leadership. Paul tells Timothy to 'Reprove, rebuke, exhort' (2 Timothy 4:2). A leader appointed by God should be a man with a mark of authority about him, especially when he stands up before a congregation to preach the Word of God. But notice that Paul adds, very significantly, 'with all long suffering and doctrine'. Not spineless, but not superior either. Beware of looking at truth just as something that God wants you to teach others. Remember that first of all it is something that God wants to teach you. Speak as a learner if you are ever going to be a teacher.

So much for James's pointed instruction – a word against carnal ambition, and a word against a critical attitude. The second thing to notice in this little passage is that there are –

2. *Powerful incentives* – 'knowing that we shall receive the greater condemnation. For in many things we offend all.'

There are two motives here –

(a) *There is a warning that our judgement is not trivial* – 'we shall receive the greater condemnation'. Now this is written to Christians. James clinches that point by linking himself into the situation; he says '*we* shall receive the greater condemnation'. But how does that tie in with the promise of Jesus that the believer 'shall not come into condemnation' (John 5:24)? Surely there is a contradiction here! Jesus says we 'shall *not* come into condemnation', and James says, 'we shall receive the greater condemnation'. Not only shall we come into condemnation but it is going to be worse for us than for anybody else. The explanation is that Jesus is using a different word from James altogether, a different word and a different meaning. There is no suggestion here, or anywhere else in the Bible, that the Christian will ever face condemnation in the sense of eternal separation from the living God. But does that mean that a Christian can be careless? We saw the answer to that in an earlier study. When a man believes and behaves with that philosophy, he is not born again. When God puts His Spirit within a man, he turns that man's will until he loves God's law and seeks to do it. He does it imperfectly, he stumbles, he falls, but he picks himself up, and sets his face once more toward heaven. Paul says 'So whether we are at home or away, we make it our aim to please Him. For we must all appear before the judgement seat of Christ, so that each one may receive good or evil, according to what he has done in the body' (2 Corinthians 5:9–10 RSV). Is not this a forgotten truth – that every Christian will stand before God and be judged? James Denney said, 'The things we have done in the body will come back to us, whether good or bad. Every pious thought and every thought of sin, every secret prayer and every secret curse; every unknown deed of charity, and every hidden deed of selfishness; we will see them all again, and though we have not remembered them for years, and perhaps have forgotten them altogether, we shall have to acknowledge that they are our own and take them to ourselves. Is that not a solemn thing to stand at the end of life?' In fact, James says more than that. He says that for those who have taken a position of authority and taught others, there will be a greater condemnation, a stricter judgement. It is clear from Scripture that as well as the division between heaven and hell, between saved and lost, there are also degrees of punishment and reward, and that those degrees depend on the light we have received, the opportunities we have had, the circumstances in which we have lived and the privileges we have been given. All of those things are going to be weighed in the mind of a perfect Judge. One may reverently say that there is a perfect sliding scale, as it were, in the mind of God, so that a cup of cold water will not lose its reward, and yet God will by no means clear the guilty. Every single Christian will spend the whole of eternity in God's presence and yet will have been accountable for every idle word that he has spoken. All will be balanced in a way that will endorse David's testimony – 'You are justified in Your sentence and faultless in Your judgement' (Psalm 51:4, The Amplified Bible). Is that not a motive that should kill at heart this striving, this carnal ambition, this longing to be superior and to lord it over people, this critical attitude, this high mindedness, this looking down at others? We are going to be judged, and there is a warning that our judgement is not trivial.

(b) *There is the wonder that our judgement is not total* – 'For in many things we offend all'. This does not mean that many things we do offend everybody. Nor does it mean the Christian is naturally an offensive sort of person. What it simply says is that we are *all* sinners, that 'we all make many mistakes' (RSV). Whenever we judge or condemn other people it is the classical case of the pot calling the kettle black, for ' we all make many mistakes'. There are no exceptions about this; notice that James again includes himself here.

In his commentary, Spiros Zodhiates points out that the phrase 'in many things' is one Greek word – 'polla', which can have these meanings – 'in many ways', 'very much', 'many times'. The Amplified Bible catches the spirit of it exactly when it says, 'For we all often stumble and fall and offend in many things'. Now do you see the incentive for not being the kind of person we exposed earlier in our study ? – the wonder that our judgement is not total – that we ourselves will not suffer the condemnation of being eternally separated from God. Try to grasp this in *personal* terms, and in the light of the day of judgement. Supposing you slip up once a day – there is one thing, one moment, one word, one attitude a day in your life that offends God. In a week that means seven; in a year, 364; in 10 years, 3,640; in 50 years, 18,200. But let us be honest, it is more than once a day isn't it ? Supposing it was once an hour. In a day, 24; in a week, 168; in a year, 8,736; in 10 years, 87,360; in 50 years, 436,800 times. Look even closer – look into the face of the Lord Jesus, into His perfect purity and honesty and love, and can you, dare you, say that you do not fall short of that glory once a minute. In a day that means 1,440; in a week, 10,080; in a year, 524,160; in 10 years, 5,241,600; in 50 years, 262,080,000! But is that the end ? No! – for the Bible says that we are all *continually* falling short of the glory of God. Moment by moment we are short of God's glory, from that point, when we are overwhelmed with the enormity of our guilt and the multiplicity of our disobedience, we can only marvel that on the day of judgement God's mercy will triumph over justice and we shall be utterly and completely without spot and

blemish in His presence for ever. As Augustus Toplady put
it

> *A debtor to mercy alone,*
> *Of covenant mercy I sing;*
> *Nor fear, with Thy righteousness on,*
> *My person and offering to bring.*
> *The terrors of law, and of God, with me*
> *Can have nothing to do;*
> *My Saviour's obedience and blood*
> *Hide all my transgressions from view.*

The Bible reminds us so clearly that 'It is of the Lord's
mercies that we are not consumed, because His compas-
sions fail not. They are new every morning: great is Thy
faithfulness.' That is it! – the wonder that God's mercies
overwhelm our sins every day! And in the light of that
truth, how should we assume any office in the Christian
church, as a Sunday school teacher, a Bible class leader, a
minister of the gospel, an elder, a deacon, a committee
member? How should we exercise that office? What should
our attitude be towards our fellow Christians? I think we
know the answer. God help us to live it out!

Chapter 9

TAMING THE TONGUE – I

*'If any man offend not in word, the same is a perfect
man, and able also to bridle the whole body. Behold, we
put bits in the horses' mouths, that they may obey us;
and we turn about their whole body. Behold also the
ships, which though they be so great, and are driven of
fierce winds, yet are they turned about with a very small
helm, whithersoever the governor listeth. Even so the
tongue is a little member, and boasteth great things.'*
(James 3:2b–5a)

We ended our last study meditating on the wonder of
God's overwhelming grace in the light of our continual
falling short of His glory. If we approach this study
rightly, that sense of wonder will increase, because James
is now about to isolate one particular area of failure – sins
of speech. The detailed development comes in the verses
covered by our next study (vv 5b–12), but this introductory
section will help us in two ways –

1. *The inference we must draw* – 'If any man offend not in
word, the same is a perfect man, and able also to bridle the
whole body' (v. 2b).

We must be sure to draw the right inference from this
statement. It is easy to draw the wrong one, because on the
surface there is a contradiction here. At the beginning of
verse 2 James says 'For in many things we offend all', but
he now goes on 'If any man offend not in word, the same is
a perfect man'. Is there not a contradiction here? Is James
saying on the one hand that we are all offending, but those
who avoid sins of speech are perfect? That would certainly
be a complete contradiction! Then can we infer that there

are some people living on earth who are perfect? Certainly
not, that too would be a wrong inference, because it would
be completely unbiblical. Three words will help us to
penetrate the surface here and get to the truth.

(1) *Mystery* – There seems to be a contradiction and
the mystery is this. It is quite clear in the first place that the
Bible commands us to be perfect. We must dare not settle
for less than that conviction. 'Thou shalt be perfect with
the Lord thy God' (Deuteronomy 18:13); 'Be ye therefore
perfect, even as your Father which is in heaven is perfect'
(Matthew 5:48). Every virtue in the Bible is commanded
and every vice is condemned. Yet the Bible makes it
equally clear that not a single person in the world *is*
perfect. Paul writes towards the end of his life, 'Not as
though I had already attained, either were already perfect'
(Philippians 3:12), and John, writing out of a long experience of walking with the Lord, says 'If we say that we have
no sin, we deceive ourselves, and the truth is not in us'
(1 John 1:8). The greatest saints outside the Bible have
confirmed these truths. No reader of Christian biography
can doubt that the closer a man gets to God, the more
conscious he is of the fact that he is falling short of God's
glory. Do you see the mystery? God is fitting the believer
for heaven, and yet the closer he gets there, the more
conscious he is of his unfitness! No amount of improve-
ment can qualify a Christian for heaven, but every Christian is absolutely certain to go there! A Christian is commanded to grow in grace, but his justification before God
does not depend in the slightest degree on whether that
growth is present or absent, vague or vigorous. Satan is a
defeated enemy, and yet he is permitted to attack the
Christian, and even to win victory after victory. The
Christian's strongest moment is when he most recognises
his terrible weakness. These things are a mystery, but
because God has sovereignly ordained them, we can only

bow in humble adoration, and recognise that in some way we cannot understand, this must be the way in which God's grace can be most magnificently displayed. Our old nature is not removed, nor is it refined. It is allowed to remain, and in some wonderful way it is by the remaining of that old nature, and by the working within us of the Holy Spirit, that God has chosen to display His wonderful grace. But let us heed two warnings here: firstly, we dare not lessen our view of what God requires in order to accommodate our weakness; and secondly, we must not slacken our efforts because God's standards are so high. Fallen nature being what it is, we are capable of both these bits of rationalisation. Now to the second word –

(2) *Maturity* – 'If any man offend not in word, the same is a *perfect* man'. But the whole drift of the passage is to show that man is a long way from perfection! – 'In *many things* we offend all' – and what James does is to take one organ, the tongue, to demonstrate the truth of what he is saying.

When I worked in the Law Courts in Guernsey I became very familiar with a document called a Crime Sheet, which listed the cases to appear before the Magistrate. It contained the names and addresses of all the accused, and also, of course, a list of all their alleged crimes. They would cover a great variety of things – one man would be accused of assaulting his wife, another of theft, another of drunkenness, and so on. On the biblical crime sheet the tongue is one of the accused and the list of offences is enormous – dishonesty, unkindness, flattery, impurity, blasphemy, pride, criticism, exaggeration, temper, greed, slander, boasting, and many others. A terrible list. What can we say about it? Two things –

(a) None of those things are impossible for any of us. I remember once climbing up to the Mount Kellogg ski slope near Pinehurst, Idaho, with a Pastor from a nearby church. As we stood watching the skiers, one of them (obviously a novice) came very gingerly down the slope and then suddenly fell head over heels right in the middle of the ski run. I turned to the pastor and said, 'You must get quite a lot of that among beginners'. 'Yes', he replied, 'and you never get so expert that you cannot do it either!' What a lesson! Let us remember that we can never get so expert in the Christian life that we are incapable of tumbling and falling in a very serious way. Let us get a realistic view of our capability of falling.

(b) Nevertheless, we should be learning. If I returned to Mount Kellogg two years later I would not expect that same man to fall in exactly the same way. I would expect him still to be capable of falling, but I would hope that he had matured, that he had grown, that he had learnt, that he had discovered the snags and areas of difficulty. And Christians should be maturing, becoming less and less ignorant of Satan's devices, more and more careful about the means of grace, learning, maturing. I have majored on this point because the word 'perfect' here could very well be translated 'mature'. Maturity is what James is speaking about. The Amplified Bible uses the phrase 'a fully developed character'. Paul tells us that we should 'in understanding be men' (1 Corinthians 14:20), and the word 'men' is exactly the same as the word 'perfect' that James uses here. In understanding be mature! God expects His children to grow, to mature, to develop. He does not expect us to make the same mistakes all the time. We ought surely to be learning. So there is mystery, there should be maturity. Now for the third word.

(3) *Mastery* – 'able to bridle also the whole body'. Some feel that 'the whole body' here means the Christian church, and that what James is saying is that a person able to control his own tongue is able to control the whole body, the church over which he is responsible. Certainly the qualification for speaking to others is not the ability to

use the tongue freely, but to use it wisely, and there is a vast difference between the two. Nevertheless, I think that the real interpretation lies elsewhere. The Amplified Bible puts this phrase – 'he is . . . able to control his whole body and to curb his entire nature'. Mastery! Control of our faculties! This is the kind of thought that James has here. We have already seen that he is not even hinting that such a perfect man exists. Yet the point he is making here is surely a very simple one. If a man really *is* able to control his tongue, then he is able to control every other part of his body, because the tongue is the most difficult part of all to control. The tongue is a very slippery customer! It is very difficult to get hold of the tongue isn't it? You can get hold of a finger, or a little toe, but to get a good grip on the tongue is much more difficult. Let me give you three scriptures which seem to suggest something very important here.

When the Lord asked Cain 'Where is Abel, thy brother', the answer that Cain gave began like this, 'I know not' (Genesis 4:9). The very first recorded words spoken by man after his expulsion from Eden were a lie. Is that any sort of indication of the proneness there is to sin with the tongue?

When Isaiah glimpsed the glory of the Lord, he said, 'Woe is me! for I am undone; because I am a man of unclean lips (Isaiah 6:5). I wonder why he said that. Was it because his lips were involved in the worst, or the most frequent of his failures?

Peter says of the Lord Jesus, 'Who did no sin neither was guile found in his mouth' (1 Peter 2:22). Now 'no sin' covered everything. Why add the reference to speech? Was it because the thing that first of all marked out Jesus was that He did not sin with His tongue?

Socrates tells the story of a simple man called Pambo who went to a wise man and asked him to teach him one of the Psalms. The wise man decided to teach him Psalm 39, which begins 'I said, I will take heed to my ways, that I sin not with my tongue . . .'. The wise man was about to go on to the next part when Pambo said, 'Wait a minute, I will go away and learn that bit'. Some months later, the wise man came across him by accident and asked 'When are you coming to learn a little bit more of that Psalm?' Pambo replied, 'I haven't yet learnt *that* lesson properly'! The story goes on, that *40 years later* Pambo gave the same answer to the same question! 'I will take heed to my ways that I sin not with my tongue' – here is a lesson which no man has fully learned, an area in which we must be seeking constantly to go on to maturity and mastery. When we have grasped that, I think we have got to the heart of what James is saying.

2. *There is an influence we cannot deny* – 'Behold, we put bits in the horses' mouths, that they may obey us; and we turn about their whole body.

Behold also the ships, which though they be so great, and are driven of fierce winds, yet are they turned about with a very small helm, whithersoever the governor listeth.

Even so the tongue is a little member, and boasteth great things.' (vv 3–5a)

James now reminds us that we cannot deny the fact that the tongue has a tremendous influence in life, and he does so in two ways. Notice two things here –

(1) *The pictures he shows.* The whole epistle of James is a picture gallery. He is a master illustrator, and this particular chapter is the most crowded room in the whole of the gallery. We have got two pictures in front of us here.

(a) *A horse controlled by reins.* That is in verse 3, which the RSV puts like this, 'If we put bits into the mouths of horses that they may obey us, we guide their whole bodies'. James's point is that something small can have a big influence. After all a bit is just a few inches long. The reins (the word might include the whole apparatus) weigh a few pounds at most, and yet that bit, those reins, can force a raging horse to turn in a certain direction. The tongue is a little thing, but for good or evil it can be a tremendous influence. That is his first picture. His second is –

(b) *A ship controlled by a rudder.* That is in verse 4, which makes much easier reading in The Living Bible – 'And a tiny rudder makes a huge ship turn wherever the pilot wants it to go, even though the winds are strong'. A ship may be new, well designed, and have a valuable cargo, but if its rudder is loose, if it is not being controlled, then that ship is heading for disaster. Positively speaking, that ship is going to be controlled by one very small rudder. So much for the pictures he shows. Now notice –

(2) *The point he stresses.* 'Even so the tongue is a little member, and boasteth great things' (v.5a). Here is the main thrust of all that he is saying here. The word 'boasteth' is not necessarily a bad word at all. The meaning is well brought out in the New English Bible – 'So with the tongue. It is a small member, but it can make huge claims'. This is not a section about the wickedness of the tongue, or its evil results, this is a section about the *power* of the tongue. The reins do not have an evil effect on the horse, and the rudder does not have an evil effect on the ship – but they have a powerful effect! So with the tongue. Its power and influence are enormous, for good or evil. Let me sum it up like this.

Firstly, the influence of the tongue can be bad. The Bible makes that crystal clear – 'Your tongue is like a sharp razor, you worker of treachery' (Psalm 52:2 RSV); 'the mouth of the wicked conceals violence' (Proverbs 10:11 RSV); 'a harsh word stirs up anger' (Proverbs 15:1 RSV). Let us not forget that! The tongue is a slitter of throats, a divider of families, a breaker of friendships, a creator of violence. Its influence can be bad.

Secondly, its influence can be beneficial. One of the

verses we have just looked at also says 'The mouth of the righteous is a fountain of life' (Proverbs 10:11 RSV). How amazingly true that is! Who can measure the goodness and blessing that has poured from the lips of God's people over the years? How much blessing the tongue has been the instrument of bringing; love, comfort, encouragement and inspiration. Again, think of all the valiant fights there have been for truth, of the people who have laid down their lives because of the things they believed, and who have uprooted tyrants from their thrones by the power of their tongue. Mary Queen of Scots once said that she was more afraid of the tongue of John Knox than of 10,000 fighting men! Above all, of course, think of the millions who have been saved, and brought into the Kingdom of God, listening to the sound of the human voice. The tongue has been an instrument in the hand of God to bring millions of people into His Kingdom all over the world down all the long centuries of time. And one final point: the influence of the tongue is an *abiding* influence. Luke Short was a New England farmer. He reached 100 years of age fit and well, and was sitting in his field meditating one day when he suddenly remembered a sermon that John Flavel had preached 85 years earlier in Dartmouth, England, before Luke Short had left for America. As he turned Flavel's words over in his mind, they came to him with such power that he was born again there and then, and became a happy Christian before he died! What a wonderful thrill, yet what a tremendous warning and challenge, that our words can have an *abiding* influence for good or for evil. No wonder Frances Ridley Havergal has a hymn that includes these words –

> *Take my voice, and let me sing,*
> *Always, only, for my King:*
> *Take my lips, and let them be*
> *Filled with messages from Thee.*

Chapter 10

TAMING THE TONGUE – II

'Behold, how great a matter a little fire kindleth!

And the tongue is a fire, a world of iniquity: so is the tongue among our members, that it defileth the whole body, and setteth on fire the course of nature; and it is set on fire of hell.

For every kind of beasts, and of birds, and of serpents, and of things in the sea, is tamed, and hath been tamed of mankind:

But the tongue can no man tame; it is an unruly evil, full of deadly poison.

Therewith bless we God, even the Father; and therewith curse we men, which are made after the similitude of God.

Out of the same mouth proceedeth blessing and cursing. My brethren, these things ought not so to be.

Doth a fountain send forth at the same place sweet water and bitter?

Can the fig tree, my brethren, bear olive berries? either a vine, figs? so can no fountain both yield salt water and fresh.   (James 3:5b–12)

This is the second part of a section dealing with the tongue, its use and misuse. James's point so far is that the tongue is powerful in its influence and effects. Now, he lists some of the things of which the tongue is capable.

1. *The tongue is capable of terrible injury.* This takes in verses 5b–8.

We have already seen that James is a master illustrator, constantly using pictures to show us just what he means.

Here, he likens the tongue to two forces, one from the natural kingdom and one from the animal kingdom.

(1) *A spreading blaze.* 'Behold how great a matter a little fire kindleth! And the tongue is a fire, a world of iniquity: so is the tongue among our members, that it defileth the whole body, and setteth on fire the course of nature; and it is set on fire of hell' (vv 5b–6).

The word 'matter' may refer to living trees or a stock of dead wood. In either case, you can see the very easy bridge between what James was saying in the previous study and the details into which he is going in these verses – 'a little fire' is sufficient to produce an enormous conflagration. During World War II I was evacuated to the Western Hebrides of Scotland, to the Isle of Islay, which seemed to me to consist of 90% heather, and a 10% mixture of porridge, herrings and scones baked on the griddle! Two other young boys were evacuees on the same farm. One of the jobs we were given was to take the ashes out of the farmhouse fire and dump them in a low lying, wet place to make absolutely sure that all the embers were put out. But as little boys our one aim was to keep them *alive* and to have some fun with them. I can vividly remember one occasion when we took one small ember from the ashes, wrapped it around with cardboard, held it cupped against the wind, and ran with it up the side of the mountain. We put the little ember down in some very dry heather and blew until it caught alight. Then we deliberately started to spread it a little bit further. We had seen heather fires put out before and we decided to see how big a frontage of fire we could allow to get going before putting it out. When we had about five yards of frontage it still looked quite small, so we let it grow to 10 yards, then 15, then 20 yards. Suddenly, that fire was raging out of control, sweeping through acres of heather with devastating speed, and I can still remember cowering in the farmhouse looking up with absolute horror as the whole of the mountain roared into flame. Every farmer for miles around rushed in to help in controlling the fire which almost literally consumed the whole mountain. As far as the eye could see there was nothing but flame and smoke. It was terrifying – and it began with a little ember that you could hold cupped in your hand! The Bible says 'A worthless man plots evil, and his speech is like a scorching fire' (Proverbs 16:27 RSV), and again 'As charcoal to hot embers and wood to fire, so is a quarrelsome man for kindling strife' (Proverbs 26:21 RSV). All of this emphasises one simple, sobering truth; the tongue is deadly dangerous, it is capable of widespread results from very small beginnings. It may well be that there should be a full-stop after the word 'fire'. Certainly we should stop and think that through the implications in our own lives. From that simple statement, James now develops the theme. Four headings will help us to get to grips with the four phrases he uses.

(a) *The suggestion of its potential* – 'a world of iniquity: so is the tongue among our members . . . '

That suggests to me the tremendous potential there is in the tongue; it is a world, and 'world' suggest vastness and variety. It is the Greek word 'cosmos' which almost invariably in the New Testament means the whole world order of things in opposition to God. John gives us a good example when he says that 'the whole world around us is under the power of the evil one' (1 John 5:19, The Amplified Bible). James's point may well be that the tongue is capable of committing, or co-operating in, every evil under the sun. Go through the Ten Commandments and you will see that the tongue is capable of committing, or sharing in, the breach of every single one of them. It is 'a world of iniquity', a microcosm of mischief. The suggestion of its potential! However let us not overstate the case. We are not saying that the tongue is specifically, or exclusively, or particularly to blame. The point that is being made is that much evil is related to one very small member, and that the tongue is capable of every kind of evil imaginable in the world. That is the suggestion of its potential.

(b) *The spread of its pollution* – 'that it defileth the whole body'. The word 'defile' comes from the root verb 'to make a stain'. The Amplified Bible uses the phrase 'contaminating and depraving the whole body'. This ties up so closely with what Jesus said – 'But those things which proceed out of the mouth come forth from the heart; and they *defile* the man. For out of the heart proceed evil thoughts, murders, adulteries, fornications, thefts, false witness, blasphemies: These are the things which defile a man . . . ' (Matthew 15:18–20). Notice how many of these involve the tongue! Just as no man can isolate himself from society, neither can he isolate one part of his body from the rest. No man can say, 'I know I have an unsanctified tongue but the rest of me is fine'! There is a spread, a stain, a seeping pollution that comes out from the tongue into every part of our body. Just as a rotten apple in a basket of good ones contaminates the rest, so you find that a contaminated tongue has an effect on other parts of our body and personality. This is why the Bible commands us 'Do not allow your mouth to cause your body to sin' (Ecclesiastes 5:6, The Amplified Bible).

(c) *The sphere of its penetration* – 'it . . . setteth on fire the course of nature'. This is the most difficult phrase in a very difficult verse. The Amplified Bible renders it 'setting on fire the wheel of birth the cycle of man's nature'. The wheel was the ancient symbol of the cycle of life, something that rolled on and on and James may therefore be saying that the tongue sets on fire the whole cycle of life from beginning to end. There is no part of life that is not touched somewhere, in some degree of penetration by what we do with our tongues.

Driving through Czechoslovakia late one night I was held up at a railway crossing. After a few minutes a goods train came rumbling through the darkness, and as it reached the level crossing, I noticed that one of its wheels was literally redhot. It was blazing, from hub to rim. I sat there mesmerised, wondering what the train's cargo was, wondering if the driver knew about the burning wheel, wondering whether somewhere along that line it might lead to disaster. At any time, at any point on the track, right until the end of the journey, that wheel of fire might suddenly produce the most terrible consequencies. Now do you see James's point about the tongue?

The tongue is used totally for communication, so it penetrates all the relationships and structures in a man's life – his friendships, his work, his home, his church. It penetrates life at every level, in every part and at every stage and it remains undiminished in its power. Notice that! The power of the tongue is as great on our death bed as it was when first we began to use it. We are capable even then of saying something that will bless and strengthen, or of flashing out something that will hurt, wound, and destroy. The sphere of its penetration!

(d) *The source of its power* – 'and it is set on fire of hell'. James is using the word 'hell' here as a synonym of the devil, in the same way that Jesus did when He spoke about Pharisees going to extraordinary lengths to make one proselyte and having done so to make him 'twofold more the child of hell than yourselves' (Matthew 23:15). Matthew Poole says, 'The tongue being the fire, the devil, by the bellows of temptation inflames it yet more and more and thereby kindles the fire of all mischief in the world'. Yet the problem is not isolated to the tongue, nor does it originate there. The tongue is set on fire by the devil. There is no answer in cutting off the tongue. The point is that the tongue is part of the totality of our personality that has been invaded by satan. James, in other words, has a realistic view of the helplessness of the human case apart from the grace of God. Theologically, this is part of the doctrine of total depravity. 'I know', says Paul, 'that in me (that is, in my flesh), dwelleth no good thing' (Romans 7:18). Isaac Watts puts it in this way in a hymn that is seldom sung today –

> *Lord I am vile, conceived in sin,*
> *And born unholy and unclean;*
> *Sprung from the man whose guilty fall*
> *Corrupts the race and taints us all.*

No wonder the tongue is capable of terrible injury! Let me just underline that word *capable* and remind you that whoever you are, whatever you have done, whatever you have been, whatever position you may hold, you are capable of the kind of terrible thing that we have seen lies inherent in the tongue. Although you may feel that there are some gross sins that you are very unlikely ever to commit, I beg of you in God's Name, to settle it in your mind that there is no sin of which you are spiritually incapable. 'Watch and pray, that ye enter not into temptation' (Matthew 26:41). The tongue is like a spreading blaze. But James adds another picture. He says it is also like –

(2) *A savage beast* – 'For every kind of beasts, and of birds, and of serpents, and of things in the sea, is tamed, and hath been tamed of mankind: But the tongue can no man tame; it is an unruly evil, full of deadly poison' (vv 7–8).

(a) In verse 7, we have a fact. In creation, God gave man dominion over all other living creatures. After the fall and the flood that same authority was confirmed. What James is doing is reminding us of these simple facts. When he uses the word 'tamed' he does not necessarily mean domesticated, nor does he mean every animal in the world. The broad truth he is stating is that human nature has dominion over animal nature and has subdued it. Man is able to pluck an enormous fish from the sea, to bring a huge animal from the forest, to strike the swiftest bird from the sky. That is a fact.

(b) In verse 8, we have a failure – 'But the tongue can no man tame; it is an unruly evil, full of deadly poison'. Do you sense the force of those three words 'but the tongue'? Man can bring under our dominion every other form of living animal creature here on the face of the earth, but the tongue, by comparison so small and so readily accessible, remains uncontrolled. Man can tame a tiger, but not the tongue! But remember again, the tongue is not to be isolated. Man is just as incapable of controlling his hands, his eyes, and his mind. The tongue is used as a symbol of man's inability which finds him crying out with Paul 'For the good that I would I do not: but the evil which I would not, that I do' (Romans 7:19). As Sir Winston Churchill once said, 'The power of man has grown in every sphere except over himself'. We can send a man to the moon, bring him back again, and forecast his landing point within yards and seconds, but we cannot tell where the tongue will travel, or where our words are going to land, where their influence is going to stop. Do you see the difference? Is that not our honest experience?

James adds two words about this failure, this uncontrolled tongue. Firstly he speaks of *its disorderly passion*. He says 'it is an unruly evil'. The word 'unruly' could be translated 'unsettled' or 'unstable' or 'disorderly'. J. B. Phillips renders the phrase 'always liable to break out'.

One of the most exciting things I can remember about life on that farm in Islay was the breaking in of a horse. For little boys it really was a terrifying experience to see a young horse brought in from the field, never having had a saddle on its back, or a bit in its mouth. Strong men would coax it into the yard and eventually manoeuvre it into a horse box. But I have seen a young horse lash and kick so violently that the horsebox just collapsed like matchwood. Here was an unruly passionate animal, and it had to be broken in. On the other hand, there was an old farm horse called Bob who was so tame and so docile that we were able to put a lump of sugar right into its mouth with no danger at all. There was no fear that Bob would ever break out again. But you can never say that about the tongue. It is an unruly evil, it is always liable to break out. Nobody is able to say, 'I am now in perfect control of my tongue, it will never let me down again, never wound anyone, never criticise anybody, never grieve the Holy Spirit'.

Secondly, James speaks about *its deadly poison*. That is exactly what he says, 'it is . . . full of deadly poison', and he echoes the Psalmist, who speaks of people with 'adders' poison . . . under their lips' (Psalm 140:3). What a shattering, humbling truth! James does not say that *certain* men's tongues are full of deadly poison. He says, 'the tongue', a generic term that includes the tongue of each and every one of us. What a responsibility we have in the whole area of our speech, remembering that 'Death and life are in the power of the tongue' (Proverbs 18:21).

This whole section has been dark and demanding. Yet we can close it on a positive note. James says 'the tongue can no *man* tame' – but Jesus can! Mark tells us how Jesus once took a deaf and dumb man aside and touched his tongue. Two verses later, we read that 'his tongue was loosed and he began to speak distinctly and as he should' (Mark 7:35, The Amplified Bible). Jesus touched his tongue! Do we know anything of that, of the Lord's daily touch on our tongue, our language?

James second main point is that –

2. *The tongue is capable of treacherous inconsistency*. This takes in verses 9–12.

It is very important to remember that when we speak of total depravity we do not mean that every part of every man is as evil all the time as it is possible for a man to be. Nor do we mean that every man is constantly committing every sin in the book every moment of his life. We have seen it to be equally true, however, that no man is constantly good and perfect in the sight of God, and it is this inconsistency to which James now turns, the fact that in his use of the tongue man can be an angel one minute and a devil the next. The treacherous inconsistency of the tongue!

Let us look at these four verses, two groups of two, in the reverse order, so that we have the illustration first and the spiritual application second. James says that this inconsistency is –

(1) *Impossible in the natural world* – 'Doth a fountain send forth at the same place sweet water and bitter? Can the fig tree, my brethren, bear olive berries? either a vine, figs? so can no fountain both yield salt water and fresh' (v. 12).

James uses another two illustrations –

(a) *A fountain.* Part of God's promise to the people of Israel before they entered the promised land was this – 'For the Lord your God is bringing you into a good land, a land of brooks of water, of fountains and springs, flowing forth in valleys and hills' (Deuteronomy 8:7 RSV). Natural springs were very common in the Middle East. Some were salt springs, some were fresh springs, but *none of them were both!* That is the whole point here – 'so can no fountain both yield salt water and fresh'.

(b) *A fruit tree.* 'Can the fig tree, my brethren, bear olive berries? either a vine, figs?' The answer is obvious. You cannot get two kinds of fruit from the same kind of tree. There is a basic law of consistency and order in nature. You can trust a spring. If it is salt water today, it will be salt tomorrow. If it is fresh today it will be fresh tomorrow, and

on neither day will it yield both together. So with a fruit
tree. It will yield the same fruit day after day. Inconsistency
is impossible in the natural world. James now goes on to
say that inconsistency is –

(2) *Improper in the spiritual world.* See how dramatically
James points out this inconsistency. He says of the tongue
firstly – 'Therewith bless we God, even the Father'. What
a wonderful way to use the tongue, the gift of speech! God
says 'Whoso offereth praise glorifieth me' (Psalm 50:23).
No wonder Isaac Watts could write

> *Sweet is the work, my God, my King,*
> *To praise Thy name, give thanks and sing*
> *To shew Thy love by morning light,*
> *And talk of all Thy truth at night.*

But James goes on to say 'and therewith (with the same
tongue) curse we men who are made after the similitude of
God'. What an inconsistency! With the same tongue praise
God, and to call down curses upon man made, as The
Amplified Bible puts it, 'in God's likeness'. Let us not play
that down. Man is not merely superior to animals. He is in
a unique relationship to God. The human race nevertheless
is the only part of God's creation which bears His image
and is capable of rebirth and restoration into His likeness.
For all his depravity man retains the dignity of being the
crown of God's creation. Yet we use our tongue to 'curse'
men. This does not mean that we literally call down a curse
upon them, but we are angry, we are bitter, we are callous,
we are critical, we use unkind words about our fellow men.
A friend once told me that one of the most challenging
sermons he had ever heard was called 'Ten minutes after
the benediction'. It spoke of those who moved in moments
from the gloria to gossip, from creed to criticism, from
praising God to wounding men. Can we plead 'Not
Guilty'? That is the inconsistency James is attacking. 'My

brethren', he says, 'these things ought not so to be.' And they ought not to be for the supreme reason that God has placed upon man an honour that he has given to none of the rest of his creation.

Does all of this expose you? Then rejoice in God's perfect answer to the problem! When the children of Israel had travelled three days in the wilderness without water they came to a place called Marah, only to discover that the waters were bitter and unfit to drink. Then we read that the Lord showed Moses a tree 'which when he had cast into the waters, the waters were made sweet' (Exodus 15:25). If you have taken this study seriously, I am sure you agree that James is not making a mistake in taking so many verses to deal with the tongue. Perhaps you have a deeper realisation than ever before that so much of your speech has grieved the Holy Spirit. Then join me in the Psalmist's prayer, not only now, but whenever the Lord reminds you of these tremendous issues – 'Let the words of my mouth. and the meditation of my heart, be acceptable in Thy sight, O Lord, my strength, and my Redeemer' (Psalm 19:14).

Chapter 11

WISDOM

'Who is a wise man and endued with knowledge among you? Let him shew out of a good conversation his works with meekness of wisdom.'

(James 3:13)

In the Wycliffe Bible Commentary Dr. Walter Wessel says 'the entire Epistle of James is wisdom literature'. That is quite a striking statement because in fact the only places where James uses the word 'wisdom' are in chapter 1 verse 5 where he says, 'If any of you lack wisdom, let him ask of God', and verses 13, 15 and 17 of chapter 3. However, we have already noticed how often James's teaching ties in directly with the Book of Proverbs, which is the great 'wisdom' book of the Old Testament.

In the verse now before us, James does two things. Firstly, he asks a question, and secondly he looks for a qualification. The question is this: 'Who is a wise man and endued with knowledge among you?', and the qualification is this: 'let him show out of a good conversation his works with meekness of wisdom'. In other words, James wants to test the claims of the kind of man he expects to find in the Christian church. He is testing the church to see whether in fact there are people there with real wisdom – and he expects to find them there! I am reminded of Paul in 1 Corinthians 6:5 'I speak to your shame. Is it so, that there is not a wise man among you?' We should expect to find people in the Christian church endued with what the Bible calls 'wisdom'. Paul is certainly shame-faced on behalf of the Corinthians that there seems to be a lack of this qualification in their church. Now it may well be that some of James's readers thought they were possessors of this gift of wisdom. It may be that verses 2–12 are in parenthesis, as it were, giving a close link between verse 1 and verse 12 – 'My brethren, be not many masters knowing that we shall receive the great condemnation . . . Who is a wise man and endued with knowledge among you'. James is going to put these claimants to the test, and so that that test can be applied to us directly, let us see the verse as making two specific demands upon us –

1. *The excellence we ought to seek* – 'Who is a wise man and endued with knowledge among you?'

This excellence is a combination of two things, wisdom and knowledge – and they are not the same. Just as there is a vast difference between cleverness and common sense, so the Bible quite clearly teaches that there is a difference between wisdom and knowledge. Cowper once put it like this –

> *Knowledge and wisdom, far from being one,*
> *Have in times no connection. Knowledge dwells*
> *In heads replete with thoughts of other men;*
> *Wisdom, in minds attentive to their own.*
> *Knowledge, a rude unprofitable mass,*
> *The mere materials with which wisdom builds,*
> *Till smoothed and squared and fitted to its place,*
> *Does but encumber whom it seems to enrich.*
> *Knowledge is proud that he has learned so much.*
> *Wisdom is humble that he knows no more.*

There is a difference between knowledge and wisdom! In fact, when we understand the Jewish conception of wisdom we will see that the difference is even greater than would appear from our modern, Western usage of the word.

Let me use two words to help break open the meaning

of this opening phrase.

(1) *Intelligence*. The Amplified Bible translates the phrase 'endued with knowledge' by the word 'intelligent'. Now obviously this does not mean a person with a high I.Q. Clearly that is not a qualification for being a Christian. However, let us not escape the thrust of this, that those who claim to teach (here is the link back with verse 1) or in any way claim to be purveyors of the truth to other people, must first of all themselves be learners of the truth. The basic qualification for teaching is learning.

While on holiday in France, C. H. Spurgeon was looking out of his hotel window watching people coming to draw water from a nearby pump. After a while he realised that one man had come again and again. Eventually he discovered the reason – he was a water seller. He was purveying it to other people, so he needed to come more often himself. The lesson is obvious. If we are going to deserve the privilege of teaching, we must apply ourselves to the discipline of learning.

But there is another lesson here. I believe that every Christian has a responsibility toward God, and, in a different way, towards his fellow men, to learn all that he can, to be 'endued with knowledge'.

Peter commands us to 'gird up the loins of your mind' (1 Peter 1:13). A Jew could not make quick progress wearing long, flowing robes. In order to get somewhere quickly he would have to pick up the fringes of his robe and tuck them into his waistband. And what does Peter say? – 'Gird up the loins of your mind'. Tuck up those long flowing robes of indiscipline, laziness, carelessness, and run for all you are worth. Get 'endued with knowledge'. No man can be a specialist in every field, and the more we discover, the more is suggested beyond our discovery. That should increase our conception of the vastness of God. We cannot know everything, but we surely should be endued with knowledge. There is no excuse for indolence, for careless preparation, for letting television do our thinking for us. Seek knowledge! God has given us the whole world as a textbook. Now to the second word –

(2) *Insight*. If knowledge can be explained or suggested by the word 'intelligence', then wisdom is explained or suggested by the word insight. Wisdom and knowledge are often linked together in the Bible: 'But where shall wisdom be found? and where is the place of understanding?' (Job 28:12); 'Get wisdom, get understanding' (Proverbs 4:5); 'Buy the truth, and sell it not; also wisdom, and instruction, and understanding' (Proverbs 23:23); 'Who is wise, and he shall understand these things? prudent, and he shall know them?' (Hosea 14:9).

Notice that wisdom is always mentioned first. That is no coincidence, because there is a real sense in which wisdom is greater than knowledge. But we must not interpret that as meaning that whereas wisdom comes from God, knowledge does not. Back in chapter 1, verse 17, James says that God is 'the Father of lights', and one of the lights of which God is the Father is intellectual light, the light of knowledge, the light of the sheer accumulation of facts. When a man learns something (I am not referring to biblical truth, that is a special area of revelation) about the material universe in which he lives, it is merely God drawing aside the curtain on the vastness of all the treasury that is, and enabling man to see part of it. Knowledge, in other words, is a gift from God. Though we do have a responsibility to learn, knowledge is still an enduement, an endowment, a gift.

Yet it is possible to have knowledge without wisdom – as the Bible succinctly puts it, 'Great men are not always wise' (Job 32:9). There is a world of difference between knowledge and wisdom. Professor Albert Einstein, the

German scientist, famous for his Theory of Relativity, said shortly before he died in 1955 – 'I feel like a man chained. If only I could be free from the shackles of my intellectual smallness, then I could understand the universe in which I live.' Here is a clue to the difference between knowledge and wisdom. Knowledge is intelligence that leaves God out, or, at least, which *can* leave God out. Wisdom is the insight that takes God in and puts Him in the very centre of the picture. That is why Solomon, given the choice of all God's gifts, cried 'Give me now wisdom and knowledge' (2 Chronicles 1:10).

The Jewish conception of wisdom was that it was God-orientated. It centred around God. As far as I can discover, nowhere in the Bible from beginning to end is wisdom used to describe an unbeliever. Now surely that is no coincidence! In biblical terms, not one single unbeliever in the world is a wise man. The Psalmist says 'The fear of the Lord is the beginning of wisdom' (Psalm 111:10) – or, as The Living Bible paraphrases it, 'How can men be wise? The only way to begin is by reverence for God'. Until a person's life is God-orientated, until it is centred upon God, he may be intelligent, but he is certainly not wise. We can therefore say there are two things about wisdom.

(a) *It begins at conversion*. One of the descriptions of the conversion experience in the Bible is that a man is 'in Christ'. Paul says 'But of Him are ye in Christ Jesus, who of God is made unto us wisdom, and righteousness, and sanctification, and redemption' (1 Corinthians 1:30). I wonder if you would have put those last four nouns in that order! – wisdom, righteousness, sanctification, redemption. Would you not tend to put 'wisdom' right at the end; after those other magnificent biblical words, 'righteousness', 'sanctification' and 'redemption'? Yet the Holy Spirit moved Paul to put wisdom first in this wonderful verse. Why? Because as soon as we come to Christ, God is put in His right place in our life, we become God-orientated, we have our first experience of true wisdom. There can never be a correct interpretation of the Bible, a right approach to life, a proper understanding of the great issues of human experience, until a man is 'in Christ'. As Paul puts it, 'Ye are complete in Him' (Colossians 2:10). Let the philosophers say what they will, the Bible's claim is no less than that wisdom puts God at the centre of things, and it begins at conversion.

(b) *It glows through communion*. The characteristic action of knowledge centres on the activity of the mind, but the characteristic action of wisdom centres on an attitude of heart. One comes through looking around, the other through looking up; knowledge extends through study, wisdom extends through meditation. Both are wonderful, because both are God's gifts. Yet there is a clear distinction between the two. It is interesting to notice the Bible's way of describing wisdom's superiority. It is 'better than ... silver and ... gold' (Proverbs 3:14); it is 'better than rubies' (Proverbs 8:11); it is 'better than strength' (Ecclesiastes 9:16); it is 'better than weapons of war' (Ecclesiastes 9:18). When Peter and John were brought before the religious and civil leaders, and gave their brave testimony, we read 'Now when they saw the boldness of Peter and John, and perceived that they were uneducated, common men, they wondered; and they recognised that they had been with Jesus' (Acts 4:13 RSV). They were 'uneducated', but they were men of wisdom, because 'they had been with Jesus'! It grows through communion. If we would grow in wisdom, we will need to heed the words of W. D. Longstaff's hymn –

> *Take time to be holy, the world rushes on.*
> *Spend much time in secret with Jesus alone.*

By looking to Jesus, like him thou shalt be;
Thy friends in thy conduct, His likeness shall see.

That is the excellence we should seek.

2. *The evidence we ought to show* – 'Let him shew out of good conversation his works with meekness of wisdom'. Now this is what we might call vintage James! The language he likes is the kind of language that can be seen so clearly, it does not have to make a noise. He is saying 'Do you claim to have wisdom, as well as knowledge? Then let me see the evidence. I can hear your words, let me see your works.' True wisdom, says James will show itself in two ways –

(1) *It will be general.* Notice very carefully that the wise man is to show 'his works'. Christianity is not just a collection of religious ideas, it is more than performing religious ceremonies. Christianity must issue in doing good. The Bible insists on good works, not as an optional extra, but as evidence of genuine faith. Will you notice also, and this is the point of using the word 'general' here, that these good works spring naturally out of 'a good conversation'. The word 'conversation' simply means 'life'. It does not mean talk, but walk, and 'a good conversation' is a life of continuing and general goodness. The trouble with some Christians is that their sudden acts of good works are spectacular because they are markedly different from their average life. There are some people who seem to have spiritual measles, they are sanctified in spots. They combine the occasional splendid with the generally carnal. Good works are not to be things we show off, but things we 'show out'! What a world of difference! True wisdom will pervade the whole life. It will be general.

(2) *It will be gentle.* James speaks of the 'meekness of wisdom'. Weymouth translates it 'a wise gentleness'. It is

something we have to *show* out, not *shout* out. 'Meekness' has been called 'the untranslatable word' and almost every translator has a different word for it. It is not just the word 'humility', it is not just the word 'modesty', although of course both of those things ought to characterise the Christian. It is Christlike for a Christian to be humble, to be modest. However, this word 'meekness' carries much more weight than that. 'Meekness' is a quality that is rooted in a conviction about the overruling sovereignty of God, and of course the perfect example was the Lord Jesus Christ. Listen to Peter's description of His meekness – 'For to this you have been called, because Christ also suffered for you, leaving you an example, that you should follow in His steps. He committed no sin; no guile was found on his lips. When He was reviled, He did not revile in return; when He suffered, He did not threaten; but He trusted to Him Who judges justly' (1 Peter 2: 21–23 RSV). That is meekness! Jesus did not assert Himself, He did not lose His temper when people disagreed, He did not trample His opponents under foot, He did not answer violence with violence, anger with anger. What a hard lesson that is to learn. We are so occupied with self, so concerned about our reputation. We dissipate so much nervous energy to fight off every pinprick that is likely to harm our pride or damage our ego. Jesus, on the other hand, was truly gentle. He 'trusted to Him Who judges justly'. That is the very heart of this word 'meekness'. In his Expository Dictionary of New Testament Words, W. E. Vine says 'The meekness manifested by the Lord and commended to the believer is the fruit of power'. Meekness is the fruit of power. The Lord was meek because He knew that He had the infinite resources of God at his command – and He says to us today 'Take my yoke upon you, and learn of me; for I am meek and lowly in heart' (Matthew 11:29).

Some years ago I came across a man I shall never forget. He was a Latvian, short, stocky, enormously strong. As a young man, while living in Siberia, he became terribly ill and vowed that if he recovered he would turn to God and give his life to Him. Miraculously his health was restored. Somehow or another he got hold of a New Testament. He began to read it, and through the reading of the Scriptures he was converted. Very soon he felt that he ought to face his widowed father with the challenge of the Word of God especially as his father was at that time living in sin with a German countess. As best he could, he told his father that he had become a Christian, and urged him to turn from his sin. His father was furious and began a terrible campaign of persecution against him. Every evening when he came in from the field his father would ask him, 'Are you still a Christian?' On getting the answer 'Yes I am', his father would order him to strip, and lie face down on the floor. He would then beat him with the buckle end of a leather belt until his back was bleeding. As he told me of this, my friend said, 'While I was working in the field I used to pray to God to help me to bear that pain without fear or resentment. And while I lay on the floor being whipped I would think of all those people who had laid down their lives for the faith, and I used to pray, "Thank you Lord for allowing me the privilege of this small sacrifice".

Now there is meekness – the ability not to use the power at one's disposal because of a conviction of God's over-ruling sovereignty. This man was one of the strongest people I have ever seen in my life, yet he allowed himself to be mutilated by a man he could have murdered. He was meek. He had learned the lesson of the Lord Jesus, and of the Apostle Peter, who wrote 'Therefore let those who suffer according to God's will do right and entrust their souls to a faithful Creator' (1 Peter 4:19 RSV).

How perfectly those two passages from Peter illustrate the meekness of wisdom, and drive home its lesson for us today! Jesus committed Himself to His Father, the righteous Judge; and Peter says we are to commit ourselves to 'a faithful Creator'. In all the turmoil which sometimes arises in your heart; in all the stresses and strains of life; in all your responsibilities at work, at home, in Christian service; in all of your attitudes towards those you are seeking to lead to the Lord; in all your reactions against those who rub you up the wrong way; in all of that network of human relationships that go to make up this thing we call 'life', hold fast to these truths – God is Creator, and so stands at the beginning of things; God is faithful, and so God stands at the centre of things; God is the Judge, and so God stands at the end of things. If we approach life with these firm convictions then we are on the high road to victory. A firm grasp of these is the foundation of true wisdom because it puts God over everything. It is the foundation of genuine meekness because it realises at one and the same time the littleness of man and the wonderful security that is his in the hand of God.

John Greenleaf Whittier captures this spirit exactly –

> *Here in the maddening maze of things,*
> *When tossed by storm and flood,*
> *To one fixed ground my spirit clings;*
> *I know that God is good.*

Chapter 12

WISDOM FROM HELL

*'But if ye have bitter envying and strife in your hearts,
glory not, and lie not against the truth.*

*This wisdom descendeth not from above, but is
earthly, sensual, devilish.*

*For where envying and strife is, there is confusion and
every evil work.'*   (James 3:14–16)

As we saw in our previous study true wisdom is God-
orientated. It begins at conversion, because no man has life
in its right perspective, until he comes to the Lord Jesus
Christ in repentance and faith and puts God at the very
centre of His life. Not only that, but it grows through communion, it develops and deepens with discipleship. Moreover, true wisdom shows itself generally in every part of a
man's life, and especially in that wise gentleness that comes
when he has a proper conception of God as the Creator
who stands at the beginning of things, as the faithful One
who over-rules the present, and as the Judge who is utterly
in control of the future of the affairs of the whole universe.
Only when we have that conception of God can we approach all of the tangled web of our human relationships
and structures in the right way. Only then do we have
wisdom in approaching life. Only then do we have that
wise gentleness that does not always have to be asserting
itself, that is not always thinking of 'here', 'now' and
'mine', but is content to rely upon God's faithfulness.

But for the very reason that wisdom *is* such a wonderful
quality, we should expect there to be a forgery. There is! –
a forgery of spiritual wisdom and James explains it in these

verses. Notice first of all –

1. *The significance of its motives* – 'But if ye have bitter envying and strife in your hearts . . . ' (v. 14). James does not begin on the circumference of our lives, not on our words or actions, but 'in your hearts'. He is concerned here with motives. It has been said that 'the heart of man's problem is the problem of man's heart', and when James begins to expose false wisdom he challenges us to look in our hearts. He does so because it is terribly, tragically, religiously possible to do the right things for the wrong reasons. James is ruthless in his denunciation of false motives, and we can see this at least three times in his epistle. He does it in chapter 2, verse 4, on the subject of discrimination; he does it here in the verse we are now studying; and he does it again in chapter 4, verse 3, where he reveals one of the reasons for unanswered prayer. Now what are the precise motives that James wants to point out here that can fester in our hearts and stain our words and our actions?

Firstly, there is *'bitter envying'*. The word 'envying' comes from the Greek word 'zelos', – our perfectly good English word 'zeal'. It is used as a good word in the Bible (in John 2:17 for instance), but in the main it has a bad connotation. In Acts 7:9, for instance, we read that 'the patriarchs, moved with *envy*, sold Joseph into Egypt'. We could use the word 'jealousy' with all of its sordid associations, and in fact The Amplified Bible does so. James, however, adds an adjective. He speaks not merely of 'envying', but of 'bitter envying', and that is a most interesting choice of phrase. The word 'bitter' is the Greek word 'pikros', from the root 'pik'. It is a picture word. It is the kind of envying, the kind of attitude, that cannot bear someone else's success or popularity and given the opportunity will humiliate and degrade them, even if it picks, even if it hurts them both.

The story is told of two men who lived in a certain city. One was envious and the other covetous. The ruler of the city sent for them and he said that he wanted to grant them one wish each, with this proviso, that the one who chose first would get exactly what he asked for, while the other man would get exactly twice what the first had asked for himself. The envious man was ordered to choose first, but immediately found himself in a quandary. He wanted to choose something great for himself, but realised that if he did so the other man would get twice as much. He thought for a while, and then he asked this – that one of his eyes should be put out.

That may be an extravagant example, but let us beware of the subtle signs. One of the most honest prayers ever prayed by a minister of the gospel, was that attributed to F. W. Robertson of Brighton – 'Lord, I would sooner your work was not done at all, than done by someone better than I can do it'. Am I wrong in calling that an honest prayer? Is it not true that even Christians are capable of descending even to that? 'Bitter envying' – is that the motive that characterises anything we do?

Secondly, James mentions '*strife*'. The words The Amplified Bible uses are 'contention, rivalry, selfish ambition'. If that is so, then we have a direct link with one interpretation of the thrust of verse 1, that we described as 'carnal ambition'. It is very interesting to notice how these treacherous twins, envying and strife, are found together in the Bible – 'For ye are yet carnal: for . . . there is among you envying, and strife . . . ' (1 Corinthians 3:3); Paul feared that when he went to Corinth he would find 'debates, envyings, wraths, strifes . . . ' (2 Corinthians 12:20); the works of the flesh include 'emulations (the Greek word is exactly the same as for "envyings") wrath, strife' (Galatians 5:20). They are found together because the Bible is true to life. A man who seems unusually concerned with the demotion of others is usually concerned with the promotion of self. The word 'strife' has a very long and tortuous ancestry, but it does seem to come out most clearly as ambition, advancement of self. Part of its history is political. It is the kind of attitude that would do anything in order to get elected. You do not have to have a very vivid imagination to carry it from politics to the church. There is the sort of man who will do anything, say anything, be anything, go anywhere, lobby anybody in order to get somewhere in the church. From there it is not very difficult to see that that can creep into so much of what we say and do. It is nothing less than the enthronement of the ego, but the terrible thing about it is that it can seem so commendable. People speak of somebody's enthusiasm, drive, initiative, but these are often just a cover up for the real motive in the heart, which is selfish ambition. Let us take the Bible's warning seriously to heart – 'the Lord is a God of knowledge, and by Him actions are weighed' (1 Samuel 2:3). God not only watches our actions, He *weighs* them, and He weighs them in scales that search the heart and discover the real motives.

That is the significance of the motives that lie behind the false wisdom. Now James goes on to –

2. *The source of its menace* – 'This wisdom descendeth not from above, but is earthly, sensual, devilish' (v. 15).

Writing on these two verses in The Expositors' Greek Testament, W. E. Oesterley says 'Nowhere is the keen knowledge of human nature, which is so characteristic of the writer, more strikingly displayed than in these verses'. Here is James really examining human nature in depth. J. B. Phillips paraphrases the beginning of the verse 'You may acquire a certain superficial wisdom, but it does not come from God'. It is not the wisdom which we can 'ask of God' (chapter 1, verse 5) because this wisdom 'descendeth not from above'.

James says three things about this false wisdom – he
describes it as 'earthly, sensual, devilish'. There are clear
links here with the unholy trinity – the world, the flesh, the
devil – and to get into the heart of what James is saying we
will need to look at each.

(1) *The world* – it is 'earthly'. Paul uses the same word
when he speaks of those 'with minds set on earthly things'
(Philippians 3:19 RSV). Here is a wisdom that is purely
earthly, its movement is horizontal, not vertical. In these
days of space travel, we could say that this wisdom is only
in earth orbit. It never escapes from the pull of earth's
gravity. As William Barclay says, 'Its standards are earthly
standards, its sources are earthly sources, it measures
success in worldy terms, and its aims are worldy aims'.

(2) *The flesh* – it is 'sensual'. The Amplified Bible translates the word 'unspiritual'. An equally good word would
be the word 'natural', which Paul uses when he says that
'the natural man receiveth not the things of the Spirit of
God' (1 Corinthians 2:14). Jude describes unconverted
people as 'sensual, having not the Spirit' (Jude 19), while
Isaiah describes the Holy Spirit as 'the spirit of wisdom'
(Isaiah 11:2). He is the only one who can give true wisdom,
clear insight, right attitudes. That is a vital point in our
Christian service and indeed in all our relationships. All
Christians have received the Holy Spirit, and every
Christian has been gifted by the Holy Spirit in one way or
another. The real question for a Christian to ask is 'Am I
using my gifts in an unspiritual way?' Remember that there
is a great difference between gifts and graces. Octavius
Winslow, in a book called *The Work of the Holy Spirit*,
writes: 'It is a remarkable fact . . . that the Corinthian
church, the most distinguished for its possession of the
gifts of the Spirit, was at the same time the most remarkable
for its lack of the sanctifying graces of the Spirit. It was the
most gifted, but at the same time the least holy community

gathered and planted by the Apostles.' What a stabbing insight that shows! Mark it carefully! – ability is no yard-stick of spirituality.

(3) *The devil* – it is 'devilish'. The Amplified Bible says, 'even devilish (demoniacal)'. The primary reference is to demons, to evil spirits, and that should cause us sobering concern. As the tide of the gospel recedes in Great Britain we are being forced, some of us for the first time in years, to recognise the forgotten facts of the presence, power and penetration of a multitude of evil spirits in the world today; spirits of impurity, hatred, atheism, disorder, rebellion and disease, and, let me add, that worldly wisdom that defies Christ and defies self. Yet all of these demons are agents of satan, the author of all sin and therefore the author of false wisdom. In fact we could call the fall of satan (if we are right in identifying it in Isaiah 14) the most overwhelming piece of false wisdom the universe has ever known. Jonathan Edwards once said, 'Although the devil be exceedingly crafty and subtle, yet he is one of the greatest fools and blockheads in the world, as the subtlest of wicked men are. Sin is of such a nature that it strangely infatuates and stultifies the mind.' We may find it amusing to hear the devil called a blockhead, but this is a matter for learning and not for laughter. Sin is the outworking of false wisdom, and false wisdom is earthly, sensual and devilish. This is the source of its menace. Now let us look at –

3. *Some of its marks* – 'For where envying and strife is, there is confusion and every evil work'. James is a great believer in the law of cause and effect. In chapter 1, verse 15, he says, 'Then when lust hath conceived, it bringeth forth sin: and sin, when it is finished, bringeth forth death'; in chapter 1, verse 25, he says, 'whoso looketh into the perfect law of liberty, and continueth therein, he being not a forgetful hearer, but a doer of the work, this man shall be blessed in his deed'; in chapter 2, verse 13, he says, 'he

shall have judgement without mercy, that hath shewed no mercy'. We have this same law of cause and effect here in verse 16. If bitter envying and strife are the motives in the heart, two results follow.

(1) There is an inward result – 'there is confusion'. There are several possibilities as to James's precise meaning here. The reference might be to rows and divisions in the church, what the Bible calls 'discord among brethren' (Proverbs 6:19). That is surely a valid interpretation, because when there is a division in a church as a result of envying and ambition, it is not 'God's work, for God is not the author of confusion, but of peace, as in all churches of the saints' (1 Corinthians 14:33). How often the Holy Spirit is given credit for something that is utterly carnal and selfish!

But another interpretation is possible. The word 'confusion' could well be translated 'instability'. It is the same kind of word that is used in chapter 1, verse 8, which speaks of a double-minded man as being 'unstable in all his ways'. There, a man's ways are unstable, here, his heart is. When a man is envious and ambitious, he can never be at rest. There is always somebody else to envy, another mountain to climb, a higher position to attain. There is an unholy restlessness about a man who is eaten up with envy and ambition.

In one of her hymns, Anna Laetitia Waring asks for '. . . a heart at leisure from itself, to soothe and sympathise'. What an insight into human nature!

(2) There is an outward result – 'every evil work'. Taken at its face value, this phrase is first and foremost a reminder that no sin is isolated or benign. Sin multiplies, it is malignant. Ambition and envy certainly are. They spread their evil throughout the whole of the Bible. It was probably through ambition that satan fell. It was through envy that Cain slew Abel. It was ambition that gripped Absalom in such a way that he stole the hearts of the men of Israel. It

was envy that drove Haman to erect what were to prove his own gallows. It was ambition that drew on the mother of James and John the disapproval of the Lord Jesus. It was envy that had a share in the crucifixion of Christ, for Pilate 'knew that for envy they had delivered Him' (Matthew 7:17). Ambition and envy spread like a malignant disease throughout the pages of the Bible, they break out again and again. And these things are written for our learning! But the primary meaning of the word 'evil' used here is not 'bad' but 'worthless'. Now that is most instructive! It is of no value. Whatever we do as the result of envying and ambition proves in the long run to be worthless. A Hollywood film star once said 'I did everything I could to get to the top of the tree, and when I got to the top I discovered that there was nothing there'. Where there is envying and strife, there is not only confusion in the heart, but a hopeless emptiness at the end of all our efforts. That is a sobering thought! When we use worldly wisdom to do God's work, when we use our own ingenuity to gain our ends or to settle our arguments in our favour, the effect of it all is uncannily disappointing. It was said of Herod that he was eaten by worms 'because he gave not God the glory' (Acts 12:23), and we will find that our enjoyment, and the effect, of our worldly efforts will just as surely be eaten away, because we do not give God the glory in these things.

There is just one more phrase in this section, the command at the end of verse 14 – 'glory not and lie not against the truth'.

James forbids two things –

(1) *Pride* – 'glory not', or as The Amplified Bible puts it, 'do not pride yourself on it'. Do not boast about anything that stems from your envy, any victory that is the result of carnal ambition, any superiority that is gained through worldly wisdom. To be envious is bad. To gain the result that you are seeking for is worse. To boast about it is the

worst of all. James forbids pride.

(2) *Pretence* – James says we are not to 'lie against the truth'. In his book *That Incredible Christian*, A. W. Tozer says, 'Hardly anything else reveals so well the fear and uncertainty among men as the length to which they will go to hide their true selves from each other and even from their own eyes'. Yet unless we are utterly out of touch with God we *know* what the real position is. The Holy Spirit reminds us. There is something unsatisfying when things are not quite right. How we should praise God for this part of the Holy Spirit's ministry!

Perhaps there is a special word here for preachers, teachers and leaders in the church. Philip Brookes once said, 'Preaching is truth expressed through personality'; how much is lost, is worthless, and gets nowhere when what a man is does not correspond to what he says! Paul asks the clinching question 'You then who teach others, will you not teach yourself? While you preach against stealing, do you steal? You who say that one must not commit adultery, do you commit adultery?' (Romans 2:21–22 RSV). We are to be what we preach. It is always easier to condemn a sin in other people than it is to conquer it in our own lives. Let us at all costs avoid pretence and hypocrisy in the pulpit! But this is true for all Christians and for every part of life. God give us grace to search in this whole area, and, when we find that which grieves Him, to repent, confess it and forsake it. In the words of William Boyd-Carpenter –

> *For sins of heedless word and deed,*
> *For pride ambitious to succeed;*
> *For crafty trade and subtle snare*
> *To catch the simple unaware;*
> *For lives bereft of purpose high,*
> *Forgive, forgive, Oh Lord, we cry.*

Chapter 13

WISDOM FROM HEAVEN

'*But the wisdom that is from above is first pure, then peaceable, gentle, and easy to be entreated, full of mercy and good fruits, without partiality, and without hypocrisy.*'   (James 3:17)

From his devastating analysis of false wisdom, James now turns to wisdom that is spiritual and godly, the kind for which we can rightly pray, and which we should seek to cultivate in our lives day by day.

First of all, he points out

1. *The contrast in this gift* – 'But the wisdom that is from above'.

The word 'but' is no accident. Coming into verse 17 is like coming into a bright sky after a storm. After all the darkness, dirt and deception of the previous verses we now come out into this wonderful atmosphere and into the wonderful virtues that we are about to have laid before us. And notice that the contrast stems from the *source* of the wisdom. 'False wisdom, as we saw descendeth not from above' (v. 15); whereas true wisdom '*is* from above'. What we might call the ingredients of this verse are not contrived, worked up, schemed for, they are not the products of our fallen nature or works of wickedness – they are gifts, or, using the word of verse 18 which is in context, they are 'fruit'. There is a similar use of words in Galatians, where Paul speaks of 'the *works* of the flesh' (Galatians 5:19), but 'the *fruit* of the Spirit' (Galatians 5:22). What a contrast! – and what a challenge, too, for every Christian should be developing this new wisdom 'that is from above'.

It began at conversion, it grows through communion. This wisdom is not earthly, it is eternal. It is not sensual, it is spiritual. It is not devilish, it is divine. What a contrast there is in this gift!

Now to the second point, which occupies the real heart of our study.

2. *The characteristics of this grace* – ' . . . is first pure, then peaceable, gentle, and easy to be intreated, full of mercy and good fruits, without partiality, and without hypocrisy'.

We could say 'the characteristics of these *graces*', because there are many of them here, but they are all manifestations of one wisdom, just as the long list of virtues in Galatians 5 are joined together as 'the *fruit* of the Spirit'. *All* of those things ought to appear in the Christian's life. *All* of them should be developed. We ought not to be sanctified in spots. As someone once put it 'Holiness is the great and fundamental law of our religion'.

When we examine the list of virtues closely, we discover that it begins with the word that describes an inward experience, and then goes on to mention seven outward expressions.

(1) *An inward experience* – ' . . . is first pure'. The Amplified Bible translates it, 'undefiled'. With unerring accuracy James puts our state before our service. He examines our heart before he looks at our hands. He is concerned about what we *are* before examining the kind of things we *do* ' . . . *first* pure'. This is an inward experience. There is an intriguing verse in the Old Testament that reads 'they made me the keeper of the vineyards; but mine own vineyard have I not kept'. (Song of Solomon 1:6). It may well be that the immediate meaning of that verse is obscure, but surely we cannot escape the underlying principle. Has God called you to be a Minister, a Sunday School teacher, a Bible class leader, an officer in the church, a committee member? Has He made you a keeper of the

vineyard, other people's vineyard? – and have you kept your *own?* Do you preach against sins that you have utterly failed to conquer in your own heart? Are you seeking to lead others into areas of Christian experience which are foreign territory to you? This is surely something of the challenge and the thrust of these words! Likewise in the verse we are studying, we are challenged to examine our own hearts, to take the temperature of our own relationship with the Lord, to check the closeness of our own walk with Him. In other words, James wants us to stop what we are doing long enough to see what we are becoming. There is a great danger in evangelical circles today of stopping short at the head and not going on to the heart. Let us remember that it is possible to feel that we know the doctrine of sanctification from beginning to end, to be able to quote all the scriptures about holiness of life, to be able to classify the fruit of the Spirit, and the works of the Spirit, the gifts of the Spirit, and all the other wonderful doctrines there are for the Christian, and still not to be a close disciple of the Lord Jesus. In writing to Timothy, Paul says 'Take heed unto *thyself*, and unto the doctrine . . . ' (1 Timothy 4:16), and a little later, 'Keep *thyself* pure' (1 Timothy 5:22). I would sooner a man was unclear about doctrine, but faithful to the Lord, than that he knew every doctrine in the book backwards and was disobedient. At the 16th Century Council of Trent, one bishop said that Protestants were 'orthodox in life, however faulty in belief'. Too often today we have got things the other way round, we are orthodox in belief but faulty in life. Beware of that!

In his book *The cost of Discipleship*, Dietrich Bonhoeffer has a section on the Beatitude 'Blessed are the pure in heart', in which he says ' "pure in heart" is contrasted here with all outward purity, even the purity of an honest mind'. That is profound! When Jesus speaks about being pure in heart He means even more than the purity of an honest mind. Listen, too, to A. W. Tozer, writing about self-crucifixion in his book *The Pursuit of God* – 'We must be careful to distinguish lazy "acceptance" from the real work of God. We must insist upon the work being done. We dare not rest content with a neat doctrine.' Do you see his point? It is not sufficient that we come away from the Bible saying that I understand perfectly what the scripture means. We must insist on the work being done, on the change being wrought, on the command being obeyed, the promise claimed. How slow we are to learn that the greatest thing we can do for the world, for our church, for our neighbour, for the work of evangelism, is to seek to have a heart that is pure from defilement of every kind.

Charles Wesley put his prayer into poetry –

> *That I Thy mercy may proclaim,*
> *That all mankind Thy truth may see,*
> *Hallow Thy great and glorious name,*
> *And perfect holiness in me.*

That is the heart of it! James says that the wisdom that is from above, is 'first pure', it is an inward experience of a close walk with God. And when there is that inward experience, and to the extent to which that inward experience grows and develops, it will find –

(2) *An outward expression* – ' . . . then peaceable, gentle, and easy to be entreated, full of mercy and good fruits, without partiality, and without hypocrisy'.

The inward experience of being 'pure' is a matter of our relationship with the Lord. The outward expression concerns relationships with other people. James mentions seven ways in which true wisdom is seen in outward expression. Let us just go through the words in turn.

(a) *'Peaceable.'* We will major on the subject of peace in our next study so let us just touch on it here. Notice firstly that it follows immediately after 'pure', exactly as it does in the Sermon on the Mount, where 'Blessed are the pure in heart: for they shall see God' is immediately followed by 'Blessed are the peacemakers: for they shall be called the children of God' (Matthew 5:8–9). The Amplified Bible translates 'peaceable' as 'peace-loving', which sounds a very comfortable, almost compromising word. But it is far from that. It is not a kind of spineless anonymity that does not want to get involved. It is not docile but diligent. It is an active seeking of the well-being of others. It means seeking to preserve peace where it exists and to promote peace where it does not exist. Some Christians seem determined to prove that they belong to the church militant by constantly fighting each other! Even when we differ on things that matter tremendously we should do so in an attitude of heart that is concerned for the well-being of our opponent – in other words we should be peaceable. Let me give just one illustration of this.

John Wesley and George Whitefield were both mighty men of God, yet on certain theological issues they were diametrically opposed. One of the issues came to a head towards the end of 1740 after Wesley had published a sermon on the subject of 'Free Grace'. On Christmas Eve 1740 Whitefield, then in America, wrote a long letter to Wesley. It was clear, firm, and decisive, and plainly showed them to be in completely opposite camps. Yet towards the end of the letter, Whitefield wrote, 'nothing but a single regard for the honour of Christ has forced this letter from me. I love and honour you for His sake; and when I come to judgement will thank you before men and angels for what you have, under God, done for my soul.' That is what it means to be peaceable.

(b) 'Gentle.' The Amplified Bible adds the words 'courteous, considerate'. A good paraphrase might be 'willing to make allowances'. To be gentle means to see the best in the worst of people, and to be moderate in our own demands. William Barclay says, 'The man who is *epieikes* (the Greek word for "gentle") is the man who knows how to forgive when strict justice would give him a perfect right to condemn.

Dr. William Trumble was travelling in a train one day when a drunken man got into his compartment. After a while he drew out a bottle of spirits from his pocket and offered Dr. Trumble a drink. Dr. Trumble responded, 'No thank you, I don't drink'. After taking some himself, the man settled back, but after a while again he took the bottle out and said, 'Go on, have a drink'. Dr. Trumble's reply was the same, 'No thank you, I don't drink'. Later, the same thing happened a third time. Suddenly, something seemed to trigger off in the man's mind. He looked at Dr. Trumble and said 'You must think I'm a beast'. 'On the contrary', Dr. Trumble replied, 'I think you are very generous.' That reply seemed to break the man's heart, and he was eventually led to Christ. Do you see the principle here? Dr. Trumble could have condemned the man for drinking. He could have quoted texts at him in a hard, bitter way. He could have walked out in disgust. Instead, he said, 'I think you are very generous'. Gentle! Courteous! Considerate! Are you like that? Or are you reluctant to forgive, to overlook, to make allowances? Are you willing to be courteous and considerate enough to see the other person's point of view. What a healing ministry this gentleness is!

(c) '*Easy to be intreated.*' Those four words are just one in the Greek, a word used nowhere else in the whole of the New Testament. Early in its history it would seem to have meant 'ready to obey'. The Amplified Bible translates it 'willing to yield to reason', while the RSV has 'open to reason'. It has obvious links with 'gentle', because it speaks of not being so dogmatic, hard and unbending, that at least you are not prepared to consider rationally what the other man has to say. During a U.S.A. Presidential Election, a man put this sticker in his car – 'My mind is made up. Don't confuse me with facts'! I do not think that we could call him 'easy to be intreated'! The Bible says 'The sluggard is wiser in his own conceit than seven men that can render a reason'. (Proverbs 26:16). What a penetrating comment! Even when seven other people can give a reason the sluggard in his own conceit thinks that his opinion is right. He is not 'easy to be intreated'. He is not open to reason. He says, 'I have made up my mind and that is it. It is an open and shut case. Nothing you can say will make me change my mind. 'In matters like this, there is a dividing line between assurance and bigotry, and we have to find out where that line is. How many churches, and fellowships, and committees are sterile and powerless because of one man who insists on his rights, who takes a rigid and bigoted line, who is not open to reason, not even open to consider the other side of the issue? Nor is the problem confined to practical matters of administration within the church. It penetrates theological issues, too. Some people are so rigid, so determined not even to listen to the other side, that they give the impression of being self-constituted arbiters of the whole counsel of God. In his book *God our Contemporary*, J. B. Phillips writes, 'Can we not be persuaded to believe that specks of consciousness on this little planet cannot, in all reasonableness, be thought of as accurate critics of the total purpose of the creation'. That is a good phrase, and its principle overspills into every area of theological dispute. Jesus never changed his mind, or took advice, or revised His opinions, or confessed ignorance on any point, but He was God incarnate. It is sad and shameful when a Christian acts as if he were an amateur Providence. Be open to reason!

(d) '*Full of mercy*.' The Amplified Bible says 'full of

compassion'. Notice the word 'full'. Compassion should
be the continuing characteristic of the Christian. James is
touching a familiar chord here. It is possible to be formal,
to be accurate and precise in our theology, to be regular
and diligent in our devotions and at public worship, to take
our full share in the work of the church – and to do so
without an atom of real compassion. I know of some
churches where the programme is run in such a cold, clini-
cal kind of way that even the work of evangelism is done
without any 'heart' at all. There is accuracy, and form, and
order, but no love, no compassion. That sort of thing was
roundly condemned by Jesus when he accused the Scribes
and Pharisees of omitting 'the weightier matters of the
law, judgement, mercy (the same word) and faith' (Matthew 23:23). The life of Jesus was a life of compassion.
As Christians, we must seek to walk the same road.

(e) '. . . *and good fruits.*' Weymouth's translation is 'kind
actions', which is exactly what we would expect James to
say! This takes us right back to chapter 2, verse 16, where
he exposes the scandal of a cold, hungry person merely
being told 'Depart in peace, be ye warmed and filled'. It is
said that an ounce of help is worth a ton of pity; we might
say here, 'an ounce of fruit is worth a ton of feeling'. It is
not enough to have compassionate feelings, we must also
have kind actions. There used to be an advertising slogan
that ran 'Where there's need, there's the Salvation Army'.
What an immense amount of James's 'true religion' is
packed in there! Whatever the need, here were Christians
prepared to help. Thomas Manton once wrote 'It is the
great fault of some that when they begin to be religious,
they leave off to be human'. A Christian should not only be
a person who is growing in his knowledge of the Lord, he
should also be the best neighbour that a man could have.
When there is an accident or sickness in the home, when
there is a hole in the roof, when a pipe bursts, or some other

crisis arises, the Christian should be the first to offer help. A Christian should be the best workmate a person could have, the best partner in business, the best social contact. And he will be if he is 'full of compassion and good fruits'.

(f) *'Without partiality.'* This is again the only New Testament use of the word. It literally means, 'not to be parted', but the RSV says 'without uncertainty', while Moffatt has 'unambiguous'. It is not a contradiction of the words 'easy to be intreated'. Perhaps it is another way of expressing what James says in chapter 2, verses 1, 4 and 9, where he says 'have not the faith of our Lord Jesus Christ, the Lord of glory, with respect of persons', and then warns his readers against being 'partial in yourselves', because 'if ye have respect to persons, ye commit sin'. To be 'without partiality' is on the one hand to be firmly closed up to God and His will, while at the same time warmly open to all the world in its need. While preaching in a church in Wiltshire some time ago, I found these words written on a plaque in the hallway: 'O God, may the door of this house be wide enough to include all who need divine love and human friendship; narrow enough to shut out all envy, pride and strife. May its threshold be smooth enough to be no stumbling block to children or to straying feet, yet rugged enough to turn back the tempter's power.' That is a fine prayer for a church – and its spirit expresses something of what James means when he says we should be 'without partiality'.

(g) *'and without hypocrisy.'* Moffatt translates this 'straightforward'. I wonder if James puts it last because hypocrisy, in one form or another, is so common. Somebody once said to Emperor Frederick III of Germany that he was going to travel to some far country where no hypocrites lived. Frederick replied that he had a very long journey, because as soon as he arrived in a country there would be at least one hypocrite there! One mark of the Bible's truth is that its heroes are painted 'warts and all';

there is even an instance of an apostle who was once guilty of hypocrisy. The question arose in the early church as to whether Gentile converts should be circumcised or simply accepted on their profession of faith, and counted as equals with the Jewish Christians. A special meeting was held at Jerusalem, and in Acts 15 their recorded verdict was that the Gentile Christians did not have to undergo the Jewish rite of circumcision. The way was open for mutual fellowship between them. Peter obeyed this ruling and met very freely with the Gentiles. He ate with them, mixed with them, and accepted them as equals. Then at some stage or another, a group of hardliners came from Jerusalem and began to apply all the old pressures about this issue. We then read that Peter withdrew and separated himself from the Gentile converts, 'fearing the circumcision party' (Galatians 2:12 RSV). In the next verse we read 'and with him the other Jews acted insincerely'. The word is 'dissembled' in the AV, and it is from exactly the same root as 'hypocrisy' here in James 3:17. The other Jews played the hypocrite with him. Now without a breath of judgement, this seems to be what happened. Peter believed that the ruling was the right one, that they ought to accept Gentile converts; but because he was afraid of the hardliners he acted as if he had changed his mind. He believed one thing, but acted as if the opposite was what he really believed. I only use this illustration to draw out one central point: hypocrisy is the sin of wanting to appear what we are not. Jesus described as hypocrites those who gave and prayed in such a way 'that they may be praised by men' (Matthew 6:2 RSV), and again 'that they may be seen by men' (Matthew 6:5 RSV).

Hypocrisy originally meant a dialogue of words, then it broadened out to mean the whole business of going on to a stage and acting a part. That is what hypocrisy really is. It is acting a part and in mentioning it here, James is back to the heart of things. What we *are* is all important. Reality will banish hypocrisy, just as hypocrisy disguises reality. It is better to be ingenuous than to be ingenious!

William Shakespeare once wrote 'This above all, to thine own self be true; then it must follow, as the night the day, thou canst not then be false to any man', and a greater than Shakespeare was able to say this, 'For our boast is this, the testimony of our conscience that we have behaved in the world, and still more towards you, with holiness and godly sincerity, not by earthly wisdom but by the grace of God' (2 Corinthians 1:12 RSV).

To live like that is to display wisdom from heaven!

Chapter 14

THE PRACTICE OF PEACE

'And the fruit of righteousness is sown in peace of them that make peace.' (James 3:18)

Although the word wisdom is not mentioned here, there is a very clear link with what has gone before. The verse could be looked at as an expansion of the first of the outward expressions of true wisdom that we saw in verse 17, which James described as 'peaceable'. Because the subject of peace is so relevant to us today in the world in which we live, I want to say two things by way of very general introduction, without at this moment touching on the verse at all.

Firstly, *peace is rare.* Is there any word in our vocabulary about which we say so much and of which we experience so little? Think of the sphere of international affairs. What a rarity peace is today! Someone has calculated that in the last 4,000 years there have only been 300 without a major war somewhere in the world. Speaking on BBC Television in December 1967, Defence Minister Dennis Healey said, 'This has been the most violent century in history. There has not been a single day since the end of World War II when hundreds of people have not been killed by military action.' We live in a world that is on fire. It is almost impossible to go through a single daily newspaper without reading of armed, violent conflict somewhere in the world. Peace is rare in international affairs.

Peace is also very rare in the world of industry. It may well be that there has never been so much machinery for negotiation, settlement and arbitration as there is in Britain today; yet major strikes in Britain amount to something like 50 a week, or 2,500 in the course of a year. People strike over pay, working conditions, their holidays and a host of other trivial issues. Not so very long ago, two swear words put thousands of people out of work for days on end. In the world of industry there is confusion and chaos. Peace is a rarity. It is interesting that a Government document produced as a possible answer to the industrial situation in Britain today was called 'In Place of Strife'. Its very title indicates the rarity of peace in the industrial world.

In the world of our community life, too, peace is rare, with people struggling for position and power. There is wrangling, in-fighting and bitterness in many of our community structures, much of it unknown to us, but reflected in our national and local press. We live in a world of teenage protest, when a cynic might be forgiven for thinking that the purpose of attending University was to hold sit-ins, or to strike, or not to eat, or to hold protest parades, or to tear the gates down; in fact to do anything else but study!

Peace is also rare in our family life in Britain. Nearly 100,000 people a year pass through our Divorce Courts and deny that bond that once they swore before God and men. And how many other families are there where there is no peace, where there is a lack of love, where there is distrust, where there is disharmony, where there is strife, unrest, misunderstanding and feuding?

And what about individual lives? Albert Camus, the French philosopher once said that every century was characterised by one special emphasis. He said that the 17th century was characterised by mathematics, the 18th century by physical science, the 19th century by biology, and the 20th century by fear. What a terrible comment on a century in which so much progress has been made in materialistic terms. Man seems incapable of stabilising himself; his life is characterised by fear and turmoil. Peace is rare.

Secondly, *peace is rich*. By that, I mean that the word is

rich in its meaning. Peace is clearly not just the absence of war. In fact, we even invented that terrible phrase 'cold war'. In other words you can have an absence of war that is so bad that in fact you must use the word 'war' to describe it! It is not just the absence of fear, conflict and passion.

There are two intriguing Old Testament illustrations of the word 'peace'. One is where we read that Joshua followed instructions to build 'an altar of whole stones, over which no man hath lift up any iron' (Joshua 8:31). The Hebrew word for 'whole' is basically the word 'peace'. These were stones that were unbroken. They were complete. No man had chipped away at them. Then in the story of the rebuilding of Jerusalem we read 'So the wall was finished' (Nehemiah 6:15). The Hebrew word for 'whole' is once more basically the word 'peace'. Here again was something that was complete. Peace is something full, rich and whole. Man without peace is not complete. He has something missing. Aristotle Onassis, one of the world's richest men, was asked on a television programme whether he had any remaining ambitions in life. He replied, 'My remaining ambition is something that is very hard to obtain, and that is peace of mind'. Peace is rich, beyond the riches of material wealth.

Now to the verse itself – 'The fruit of righteousness is sown in peace of them that make peace'. These few words have raised many problems of interpretation. Is this 'fruit of righteousness' something we obtain on earth, or does it await the Christian in heaven? Is this *fruit* the result of righteousness, or is it in fact the thing of which righteousness *consists*? Is peace the seed that we sow, or is it the object of sowing the seed?

I see this verse as speaking of the wise man's responsibility on the subject of peace and the result of his exercising it, or more simply, the Christian and peace. Let us take the phrases in the reverse order.

1. *The Christian's approach* – 'them that make peace'. Peace is something that needs to be made, it is not something that exists naturally in the fallen spiritual world. No virtue does! I was at a Christian conference once when about £1,000 worth of electronic equipment was stolen on the first night we were there (not, I trust, by Christians!). The council and team responsible for the Conference not only informed the Police, but also met to pray about the matter. When we had finished praying, one of the council members said, 'I just want us to get this thing in its right perspective. Let us not be *surprised* that this stuff has been stolen. I am a director of a building firm and we accept it as standard practice that pipes, timber, bars, sinks and a host of other things will regularly disappear from our building sites. *This is standard practice in the kind of world in which we live today.*' That was pretty sobering! – but completely realistic! Honesty is not natural. Neither is peace. Notice, too, that the language is not academic. Peace is something to be made, to be worked at.

Can you imagine a farmer spending all his time in an armchair, reading glossy magazines about the best seeds and the best fertilizers and the best way to gather in the harvest? He would have little to show for it if he did! If he is to have a harvest, he must work for it. It is an interesting coincidence that every single chapter in James's epistle ends with an insistence upon good works, upon doing something. The reason is obvious, as we have already seen. It is by good works that a man proves the reality of his profession of faith. Jesus said, 'Blessed are the peacemakers: for they shall be called the children of God'. We do not *become* the children of God by being peacemakers, but when we *are* peacemakers, when our lives are going out to produce peace, then we *prove* ourselves to be the children of God, we earn the right to the title. Peacemaking is not just a doctrine, it is a duty.

Let us look at three things about the Christian's approach to peace.

(1) *He should preserve it.* Paul says, 'Let every soul be subject unto the higher powers' (Romans 13:1). Here is a word about our civic responsibility. A Christian should readily and happily obey the civil authority that is placed over him, unless it is in direct conflict with the law of God. Paul also says that we are to live 'with all lowliness and meekness, with patience, forbearing one another in love, eager to maintain the unity of the Spirit in the bond of peace' (Ephesians 4:2–3 RSV). Whatever disagreements he might have with another person, a Christian is bound over to keep the peace!

(2) *He should promote it.* Let me put this in the form of a question. Does the general flow of your life tend to promote peace, or do you tend to be prickly, touchy, and difficult to get on with? Does your life tend with gentle firmness to remove evil and to replace it with good – and to do so in a peaceable way? Abraham Lincoln once said, 'I would like it to be said of me that I always pulled up a weed and planted a flower where I thought a flower would grow'. We should not only be peace-lovers, but peace-livers, the kind of people who promote peace by our general attitude and approach.

(3) *He should pursue it.* I am struck by the way the Bible uses exactly that sort of word again and again. Here are four examples, quoted from The Amplified Bible for the sake of emphasis – 'Depart from evil and do good; seek, inquire for and crave peace, and pursue-go after-it!' (Psalm 34:14); 'So let us then definitely aim for and eagerly pursue what makes for harmony and for mutual upbuilding (edification and development) of each other' (Romans 14:19); 'Be eager and strive earnestly to guard and keep the harmony and oneness of (produced by) the Spirit in the binding power of peace' (Ephesians 4:3); 'Strive to live in

peace with everybody . . . ' (Hebrews 12:14). That is un-compromising stuff, and someone may want to seek refuge in Romans 12:18 where Paul says, 'If it be possible, as much as lieth in you, live peaceably with all men'. But far from excusing us, surely that verse examines us. The RSV renders the opening phrase 'If possible, so far as it depends upon you'. This does not excuse us from seeking peace, it asks whether we are in fact pursuing it with every power at our disposal. Jesus said of the woman who anointed Him with spikenard in the house of Simon the leper at Bethany 'She has done what she could' (Mark 14:8 RSV). Could that be said about you in the matter of your relationships at your church, at work, on committee, or there in the home? Are you doing all you can to pursue peace? Are you willing to sacrifice everything except principle in order that there might be peace in that situation? There are at least three specific things on which the Bible speaks to us here –

(a) *Our relationship with God.* This matters most of all. Now you would almost begin to expect that from James. Eliphaz advised Job 'Agree with God, and be at peace; thereby good will come to you' (Job 22:21 RSV). This matter of agreeing with God, of Job's walk with the Lord, was not just something internal and subjective; it was out-working and practical. By what a man is in his life, he contributes either to peace or to strife. Inward peace is something that naturally works out into its immediate surroundings. There is nothing more practical than a man's walk with God. When a man is at peace with God, he has a wonderfully therapeutic effect on his personal relationships and on the atmosphere in which he lives. The Bible says 'Thou wilt keep him in perfect peace, whose mind is stayed on Thee: because he trusteth in Thee' (Isaiah 26:3), and Frances Ridley Havergal put the thought in to these magnificent words –

Like a river glorious is God's perfect peace,

Over all victorious in its bright increase;
Perfect, yet it floweth fuller every day
Perfect, yet it groweth deeper all the way.

Hidden in the hollow of His blessed Hand,
Never foe can follow, never traitor stand;
Not a surge of worry, not a shade of care,
Not a blast of hurry touched the spirit there.

Stayed upon Jehovah, hearts are fully blest,
Finding as He promised, perfect peace and rest.

If you want to pursue peace, to be an influence for peace, to be the kind of person whose very presence in a situation has a healing effect, you begin in terms of your own personal relationship with God.

Not only our relationship with God, but –

(b) *Our responsibility to the Gospel.* Christians are 'ambassadors for Christ' (2 Corinthians 5:20), and among the other duties of an ambassador is the passing on of messages from his ruler or sovereign. Exactly the same thing is true about Christians. Our role as ambassadors for Christ is not seen in context until we link the verse in which the words occur with the previous two verses – 'And all this is from God, who through Christ reconciled us to Himself and gave us the ministry of reconciliation; that is, God was in Christ reconciling the world to Himself, not counting their trespasses against them, and entrusting to us the message of reconciliation. So we are ambassadors for Christ' (2 Corinthians 5:18–20 RSV). Evangelism is the pursuit of peace! In his book *Let me Commend*, Dr. W. E. Sangster describes it as 'the sheer work of the herald who goes in the name of the King to the people who, either openly or by their indifference, deny their allegiance to their rightful Lord. He blows the trumpet and demands to be heard. He tells the people in plain words of the melting clemency of their offended king and of the things that belong to their peace.' The gospel brings peace between God and man and also between man and his fellow-man.

In the early 1960s Nigeria was a bloodbath, as tribal, social and political hatreds erupted into violence and the most terrible atrocities. Yet in 1962 the officers of the Scripture Union in Nigeria were drawn from three opposing tribes; the President was a Hausa from the North, the Secretary was an Ibo from the East, and the Chairman was a Yoruba from the West! The gospel brings peace, and if we are concerned to pursue peace we must be involved in the work of evangelism. One of the Bible's loveliest descriptions of evangelism is 'preaching peace by Jesus Christ' (Acts 10:36). Our relationship to God, our responsibility to the gospel, and then –

(c) *Our reaction to godlessness*. The Bible makes this so clear. 'A soft answer turns away wrath, but a harsh word stirs up anger' (Proverbs 15:1 RSV); 'Deference will make amends for great offences' (Ecclesiastes 10:4 RSV). 'Put on then, as God's chosen ones, holy and beloved, compassion, kindness, lowliness, meekness and patience, forbearing one another and, if one has a complaint against another, forgiving each other; as the Lord has forgiven you, so you must also forgive. And above all these things put on love, which binds everything together in perfect harmony' (Colossians 3:12–14 RSV). Two of the loveliest biblical examples of that kind of behaviour are seen in David's treatment of Saul. David had two great opportunities to destroy Saul, but in both cases he spared his life. After the first incident, even Saul admitted, 'You are more righteous than I; for you have repaid me good, whereas I have repaid you evil' (1 Samuel 24:17 RSV). David's reaction to godlessness, bitterness, reproach and opposition from Saul was to pursue peace. No wonder God called David 'a man after mine own heart' (Acts 13:22). Paul says in Colossians 1:21 that although we were once 'alienated and enemies in your mind by wicked works' we were nevertheless 'reconciled in the body of (Christ's) flesh through death'. Again, he reminds us that 'Christ died for the ungodly' (Romans 5:6). God's reaction to our godlessness was to pursue peace even at the cost of the blood of His own Son. To grasp this is to understand more clearly the words of Jesus, 'Blessed are the peacemakers: for they shall be called the children of God' (Matthew 5:9). Every time we are offended, reviled, wronged, abused, criticised or slandered, we have an opportunity to be peacemakers; and the greater the sin the greater the opportunity of demonstrating the goodness of God, and the grace of God in our own lives. 'Do not be overcome by evil but overcome evil with good' (Romans 12:21 RSV).

So much for the Christian's approach to peace, which now mingles with –

2. *The Christian's attitude* – 'is sown in peace'.

The New English Bible translates this 'is sown in a spirit of peace', and this may well catch the meaning here. The fruit of righteousness is sown *in a spirit of peace*. Those words are important! It is possible to preach the gospel in a militant, bitter, critical kind of way. Two ministers were having a conversation one day when one asked the other 'What did you preach on last Sunday?' His friend replied 'I preached on "The wicked shall be turned into hell" .' The first minister then asked 'Did you preach it tenderly?' We must sow in a spirit of peace! Perhaps we can add two points here:

(1) *We should be courteous all the time.* A man called John Dickenson used to live in Birmingham, and he was known as 'the Peacemaker'. It was said of him – 'such was his anxiety to keep the bonds of peace from being broken ... and to heal the breach when made, that he would stoop to any act but that of meanness, make any sacrifice but that of principle, and endure any mode of treatment, not excepting even insult and reproach'. The Christian should be

courteous all the time. As James puts it 'for the anger of man does not work the righteousness of God' (James 1:20 RSV). In this, as in everything else, we must practice what we preach. We are not worthy ambassadors of a gracious and loving God if we are critical, harsh and bitter in our Christian life and service.

(2) *We should be conscious of the time.* Not only courteous all the time, but conscious of the time. Thomas Manton wrote 'Have a care of the season; it is seed-time', and of course he was right. All of life is a kind of sowing. Our activity is sowing, and so is our inactivity. The good things that we do and the bad things too, all are sowing. It is seed time, today is seed time, tomorrow will be seed time. For young people, it is seed time; for those in the middle of life, it is seed time; for those in the latter years, it is seed time. All of life is sowing. And how many more handfuls of seed do we have left to sow? Nobody knows. Seed-time is an urgent time, a limited time. Is there an apology you ought to make? A letter you ought to write? A restitution you ought to see to? A hand you ought to offer? A misunderstanding you ought to correct? A gift you ought to make? Then *do it!* and do it quickly, because it is seed time, and 'night comes when no one can work' (John 9:4 RSV). We are to sow in peace, courteous all the time, conscious of the time. Those two thoughts are wonderfully taken up by Paul when he says 'Walk in wisdom toward them that are without, redeeming the time. Let your speech be alway with grace, seasoned with salt, that ye may know how ye ought to answer every man' (Colossians 4:5–6). That is the Christian's attitude. Finally, let us notice –

3. *The Christian's aim* – 'the fruit of righteousness'. The RSV translates that, 'the harvest of righteousness', and that is the sense in which I shall interpret it. The word 'righteousness' used to be spelled 'rightwiseness'. It means the wisdom of living rightly, in conformity with the will of God. As we come to the close of this study, it might help to

attempt a paraphrase of the whole verse, as follows: Those who seek to make peace in a peaceable way, produce a harvest of righteousness in themselves and others. That seems to me to be the sense of the verse. The aim is not just peace. It is certainly not a question of peace at any price; true wisdom, as we have seen, is 'first pure', and the Bible says that we are to 'Follow peace with all men, *and holiness*, without which no man shall see the Lord' (Hebrews 12:14). We are not to be peacemakers at the expense of truth. There is such a thing as the sin of tolerance.

Notice also, that James uses the language of faith here – 'The fruit of righteousness is sown in peace'. He does speak of 'seed' being sown, but 'fruit'! He is sure of the outcome. It is the language of faith – ' . . . one who sows righteousness gets a sure reward' (Proverbs 11:18 RSV). There is a sure relationship between what we sow and what we reap. That law is woven into the very fabric of God's Word.

Finally, notice that although the Bible commands righteousness as an aim, it is not righteousness in a vacuum, but only righteousness as it is wrapped up in the greater aim of the glory of God. That is the point at which we should close this study. In a wonderful Messianic chapter, which also speaks of the church, the Lord's work in the hearts of His people is said to be 'that they might be called trees of righteousness, the planting of the Lord, *that He might be glorified*' (Isaiah 61:3).

Anna Laetitia Waring gives us just the right prayer in these words from one of her hymns –

> *I ask Thee for the daily strength*
> *To none that ask denied,*
> *And a mind to blend with outward life,*
> *Still keeping at Thy side,*
> *Content to fill a little space*
> *If Thou be glorified.*